Written R.

Lewis

Either
Everything
Was
Wrong
From The Git
Go Or Right From
The Start

*Written by*
**Debbie Lynn Lewis**

*Illustrations by*
Sharon Bourgeois

*Cover by*
Jamavia Bourgeois

*Arranged by*
Alexander Bourgeois IV/ Debbie L. Lewis

**Either Everything Was Wrong from the Git Go or Right From the Start**
Copyright © 2019 by Debbie Lynn Lewis

All rights reserved. No part of this publication may be reproduced, distributed, or transmitted in any form or by any means, including photocopying, recording, or other electronic or mechanical methods, without the prior written permission of the publisher or author, except in the case of brief quotations embodied in critical reviews and certain other noncommercial uses permitted by copyright law.

Although every precaution has been taken to verify the accuracy of the information contained herein, the author and publisher assume no responsibility for any errors or omissions. No liability is assumed for damages that may result from the use of information contained within.

Library of Congress Control Number: 2019940954
ISBN-13: Paperback: 978-1-64398-798-9

Printed in the United States of America

LitFire
PUBLISHING
LitFire LLC
1-800-511-9787
www.litfirepublishing.com
order@litfirepublishing.com

# Contents

CAST ................................................................. v

Treatment ............................................................ 1

Opening of the movie ................................................. 3

About the Author ................................................... 123

# CAST

| Characters | Age(s) |
|---|---|
| Lady JoAnne Lewis-Charlatan | 54-60 |
| Trish Arlene Spears | 23-30 |
| Bece (Bryce) Jones | 16-17 |
| Siddy Alex Larue | 48-52 |
| Cindy "Chocolate" Dee Charlatan | 30+ |
| Eeshun Latrelle Wells | 30 |
| Pete Sharron-Renê Rosalyn | 23-30 |
| Tiggs Levette | 25-30 |
| Woody Pitts | 16-17 |
| Beep Mabry | 16- 17 |
| Devin Zzavier Waters | 8-10 |
| Melody Bertha Waters | 28-32 |
| Day Mario Beens (Benz) | 30 |
| David Derrick Clearly | 60 |
| Like Demerris Waters | 30 |
| Bart (Bartholomew) Carson Jones | 25-30 |
| Reverend James Holt | 50-60 |
| Receptionist (Triplets) (Ericia, Audrey, Latrice) | 30 (-+) |
| Waitress (Florence) | 23-27 |
| Black Helper (Warner) | 33-40 |
| Day's Mom (Jean) | 40 |
| Eeshun's Father (Land) | 40 |
| Lady's Teacher (Joyce) | 40 |
| Principal (Mayden) | 40 |
| Janitor (Keith) | 40 |
| Chorus/Graduation Teacher (Deborah) | 40 |
| Little Lady | 7-9 |

# Treatment

Cindy "Chocolate" Charlatan Jones:(Now) Serious, Horny, Bright and Grieving, this is all mixed up in one package. Cindy's high school years: (Then) Distant, Very Smart, Almost on the dark side, and very passionate about her beliefs. Wasn't a trouble maker, but wasn't good at taking orders from anyone either. Determined and strong minded too. You could always find her wearing black.

Eeshun Wells: (Now) Very Stylish, Outgoing, Witty, and uncouth. Eeshun's high school years: (Then) Loyal, Adventure Seeker, and not understood by her fellow peers, pretty much only Cindy understood her. Stayed in Atlanta while Cindy ventured out in acting and she became the top hair stylist in Georgia with her own hair care product line.

Bece (Bryce) Jones: Good sense of humor, covering up true feelings. Perfectionist, but really don't mean to be. Lie, he thinks it will upset his momma if he wasn't good. Looking out for his momma and is worried about her wellbeing.

Like Waters: Charming in manners, Quiet until spoken to, then he talks your ear off. Torn. A loving family man with a strong passion for music.

Pete Rosalyn: Shy, Non-chalant, secretive, but is very good with a pair of drumsticks. Tired of being a fetch boy.

Trish Spears: Delvish, on a mission to produce the best sound track ever. She's not a mean person. She has a nice nasty, professional business lady mentality about her. She will get the job done.

Day Beens: Trying to retire, but really don't want to. He just needs something to hold on to. Cheerful, out looking for love and trying to hold on to the love of music.

Lady Charlatan: A very determine woman, who is feed up with the bullshit of the world. She's a loving grandmother and mother. With a lot of things to get off her chest. Will she?

David Clearly: He's a good man still waiting on his chance.

# Opening of the movie

We see a plane in the sky. Now we are on the plane, as the airline stewardess approaches Cindy, she begins to speaks.

Stewardess:
Excuse me would you like soda or water?

Cindy:
(She has on earphones. Then the stewardess taps her.) Oh, yes! (Startled at where she is.)

Stewardess:
Soda or water?

Cindy:
Neither thank you. (Stewardess passes on. Cindy begins to look around. She knows she's on a plane, but why? She gets up and begins to walk towards the back. She notices a lot of people. Pasty Cline, John Brown, Buddy Holly, Ritchie Valens, J.P Richardson, Ronnie Caldwell and Otis Redding, then she sees Bartholomew "Bart" Carson Jones in the back (her husband) She starts to walk towards him; then she looks to the right and she sees John F. Kennedy Jr. with two ladies talking. She walks up to them.) Excuse me Mr. J. Jr. Are you…?

John F. Kennedy Jr.:
(He cuts her off.) It's not your turn (then turns his head.)

Cindy:
Uhh, what excuse me (then the plane starts to head dive pretty fast and Cindy awakens.)
* Note we don't hear any screams.*

"Either Everything Was Wrong From the Git-Go or Right From the Start"

*(In Cindy's bedroom. She's on the phone.)*

Cindy:
Yes, mom I'm still going tonight. Will you please stop with the same question already? I said I was going so I'm going okay. Now let me get my day started. You have a good one too, Love ya. Bye.(still a little baffled about the dream, hangs up phone. )

Bece:
You okay in here? (Cindy not really listening.) Are you still going with Auntie "E" tonight?

Cindy:
Yes, I'm still going. Why is everyone checking up on me? I'm all right.

Bece:
Sorry, Sorry... Well may I see your car keys?

Cindy:
(Knowing exactly where this is leading to.) What's wrong with your car Bece?

Bece:
It's at Wood Tech, I'm letting some of the boys put a stereo in for me. So can I borrow your keys?

Cindy:
You mean my car with my keys?

Bece:
Mom you know what I mean.

Cindy:
(Soft hearted) Yes you can. Get them off the T.V.

Bece:
(Grabs the keys and leaves the room.) Love you mom, see ya!

*Now we find ourselves across town at one of the city's finest night spots The Ying Yangs. We find the "The Best Boys in Town" Band at rehearsal. (Aa 1, Aa 2, Aa 1 , 2, 3, 4 is heard over a loud speaker.)

Big Guss:
Something is wrong with my mic.

Like:
What could be wrong with your mic?

Big Guss:
It's too close.

Like:
Well move it back Big Guss (Looks around.) Where is Pete? (Band members are goofing off as usual.) Where is Pete?

Tiggs:
He's gone to pick-up the guest bass guitarist, um Mr. Day Beens. (Band members still goofing off.)

Like:
Damn it, What is up with everyone around here? (They stop and listen.)We have a big gig tonight and I want everybody playing like it's his last gig in life.

Tiggs:
Waters you know that's basically how we play every night. Just chill it's going to be all right.

Like;
Okay maybe you're right…

Tiggs:
I am.

Band Members:
He is!

Like:
Don't push it. Aa 1, Aa2, Aa3 (Then band starts to play an up tempo song. Like Waters's son Devin comes over and taps him.)

Like:
What is it son? (As a caring father.)

Devin:
I'm thirsty and I need to go to the bathroom.

Band members:
(Laughs )

Like:
Don't laugh it's not funny. (Escort Devin to the bath room.)

(Trish Spears enters club. She takes a seat in the back and is checking out her surroundings. Bartender comes over to Trish.)

Bartender:
Excuse me ma'am, I'ma have to ask you to leave. This is a closed rehearsal to the public.

Trish:
I was invited.

Bartender:
Usually it's open to the public, but this is a special night. So I'ma still have to ask you to leave and come back tonight. I'm quite sure you'll find the band is up to par.
(Trying to assist Trish up & out.)

Trish:
But sir,...

Bartender:
(cuts her off.) Here are some complementary drink tickets. I'll remember you tonight I promise. (Then he winks at her.)

*(By now Trish and the bartender are at the door and
Trish refuses to debate the issue any longer.)*

Trish:
(Peeved but under control.) Thank you very much sir. (Takes the tickets and walks out.)

Like:
(Returns just as she is leaving.) Ready... This is a big night, I've invited a lot of important people out tonight.

**\*-SWITCH-\***
*You can't break friends up they can only break up.*

Cindy:
Thanks for coming to get me. I can't believe that boy, he took my car to get his car and now he's making me come back to my old high school grounds to retrieve my own car .

Eeshun:
No problem girl. I was kinda glad you called, it gave me a reason to visit the school too. I haven't been back for twenty years. You remember when?

**\*Time Switch-\***

*(1977, In chorus.) We met in chorus when we paired
up in-groups, you were a little nerdy then.*

**\*Time Switch 1999 for one second\***

Cindy:
(Recalls too.) I wasn't nerdy, I was expressing myself Thank you very much and black was my favorite color at that time.

Eeshun:
Yeah, Yeah, Yeah whatever may I finish my story please?

Cindy:
(Waves her hand for her to continue.)
Continue.

Eeshun:
We were working on the alto part and your mind kept drifting or shall I say it was gone. (They both laugh with their heads down. When they lifted their heads back up time has switch back to 1977 in chorus room.)

*(Chorus members in place in chorus/band room singing. Cindy is looking across the room over into the boys' section and Eeshun is putting on lipstick, when a new student walks in. He walks up to the piano, the teacher stops playing it. They exchange some words to each other, then the teacher announces to the class.

Teacher:
Excuse me class we have a new student by the name of Day Beens. He's from Chicago so please give him a southern welcome.

Students:
(They do different kinds of welcomes. Some clap, whistle, holler etc...)

Teacher:
Day go have a seat in the boys section and we'll figure out which section you really belong in later. Bass or tenor? (Day shrugs his shoulder.)

Eeshun:
Oh my goodness do you see that kid? He is fine as hell. C-C are you listening to me?

Cindy:
What's wrong with everyone in here?

Eeshun:
There's nothing wrong.

Cindy:
Why are we all separated?

Eeshun:
What are you talking about? The whole class is here today plus an extra new kid.

Cindy:
No, No look around us Eeshun we are all separated. Look Day broke the cycle. (Day is standing with the white kids.)

*(Back to the present time 1999.)*

Eeshun:
We are here!

Cindy:
(Looks around) Girl, nothing has change.

*Fade-out*

*When it's time to switch shifts you want everybody in their place on time.*

Like:
Honey I'm home. (We see Devin run to his room. The phone rings, but he will not answer it. He speaks to himself out loud)
Everybody knows how I am before a big gig. I don't want to talk because usually it's bad news and that gets me all worked up. (Answer machine picks it up. Beep sound)

Melody:
Hi honey it's me. I know you're home so I'll just say what I have to say. I'm not coming to your show tonight, I'm not cooking dinner tonight either. What I'm really trying say is I need some time to myself... So I'm not coming home either. I'll call you later. (Beep)

Like:
What just happen here? Did I miss something? She'll call me later. What the____!?

## *-SWITCH-*

*We may start off on one road and end up on another or
is it the road we really suppose to be on?*
*(We see Day at an airport, but it's not Atlanta, it's in Mississippi.
He's trying to get an answer at the club, but no one is there. We
see Pete stuck in traffic with hardly any gas. He's pissed.*)

*(Trish Spears is in her office telling her boss what happen and
she really don't want to go back to the club tonight.)

Trish:
Yes Mr. Clearly the band was there, (on the phone.) but I didn't speak to anyone. The bartender kicked me out so fast, I didn't even have a chance to explain who I was. No sir no one tried to stop him. You are right maybe no one really knew who I was, but... Yes, Yes I know, but, but Mr. Clearly. I have a really bad headache and I'm not up for a loud band tonight. Will it be okay if Charles take my place tonight? Okay. Bye.

## *-SWITCH-*

*Time is precious so don't waste too much of it.
*(In the schools mechanic shop with the radio on.)*

Bece:

I don't believe this, you can't even put a simple stereo system in. I only have four (4) woofers, two (2) twitters, two (2) door speakers and one (1) sixty (60) CD player by Toshiba and you are destroying it. Move, move I'll get it!

Woody:

Dog man you don't have to be so hasty about it…

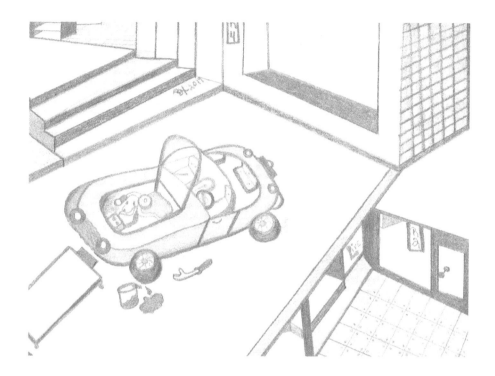

Beep:

We told you anyway that this is going to take some time.

Bece:

I thought you meant hours because it was so much. Not days because you had to read the manual to figure out which way to turn the speakers.

Woody:

Just chill man and pass me that wrench.

Bece:

What do you need a wrench for?

Beep:
I think we hit a pipe or something and green stuff is leaking out.

Bece:
This can't be happening. I have my mom's car can you guys tell me when you can have my car back to one piece again?

Guys:
I don't know.

*It's funny how places can bring things back to mind.*

Cindy:
Oh my goodness, It's still the same around here Eeshun.

Eeshun:
I know. They haven't even upgraded the pictures on the wall.

Cindy:
(Acting out a male teacher's voice.) There's a lot of history down these halls, one day you shall make your own history.

Eeshun:
(Laughs with all her might.) I believe there's been new history since then.

***Time switch 1978*** 

Mr. Rogers:
(Cindy and Eeshun laughing in hallway)
Excuse me young ladies what are you doing here? Shouldn't you be in detention?

Cindy:
No sir we have a hall pass and we are taking some papers to Mrs. Milton.

Mr. Rogers:
It takes two of you to take papers to Mrs. Milton?

Eeshun:
Yes sir she's new and I'm showing her around the school.

Mr. Rogers:
Continue on (Knowing they are not telling the truth.) you only have five minutes and I'm watching you two.

Girls:
(Runs down the hall.)

Mr. Rogers:
No running!

***-Time switch-***

( NOW at the same time in 1999 they are running down the hall. They bump into the school's janitor.)

Girls:
Excuse us we're looking for the mechanic shop?

Janitor:
(He just points downstairs.)

Eeshun:
Thank you!

Cindy:
I told you nothing has changed.

*Fade Out*
*(Across town life is still going on.)*
*Magnolia Room For Fine Dining

As we enter, the atmosphere is dark, the furniture is burgundy. We have classy and antique combined in this well - known establishment. In the dining area they are having a luncheon with some of Atlanta's big spenders. As we cut to the kitchen we see workers moving fast and it is a little chaotic back here to make sure everything run smoothly.*

Lady Charlatan:
Please remove the Cornish hens out the oven. Someone needs to get the white dollies out and I can't find my giant tongues.

Waitress:
Everything is looking so good out there, Lady C. everyone is smiling, eating and being merry all because of you.

Lady:
Stop it girl.

Waitress:
I'm serious. I've only heard wonderful things about your food.

Lady:
Well maybe this time Mr. Larue will let me come and take a bow. That's only if he's not in one of his moods.

Waitress:
I know what you mean. One of his, I've done this all by myself moods.

Lady:
Selfish prick.

Mr. Siddy Larue:
(Comes into kitchen.) I think everything is going swell.

Waiter:
Once again Lady has pulled off another magnificent meal. (The workers give her a hand.)

Mr. Larue:
Cease, enough small talk lets keep on working people. We have rich clients out there today and they might come back yearly If I can pull this deal off.

Waitress:
Are they tipping today?

Crew:
(Laughs)

Mr. Larue:
(Claps his hands as to say )

Get back to work. (Then walks over to Lady.) Try not to brown the bread so much. We like light bread and don't put too much food on their plates. (As he says this he is picking food off their plates with his hands. Then he walks out the kitchen. And the crew looks on.)

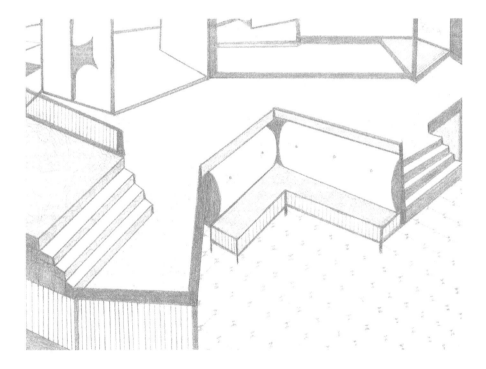

Lady:
(Trying not to show her feelings she looks at the crew then orders.) Someone please take the bread out the oven and remove some of the food off the plates.

**\*-SWITCH-\***

*Some things don't always look like what it seems.*

Tiggs:

(Comes into his house picks up some pants off the floor, then see some woman's panties on the floor. He picks them up and smile. Looks at the clock and it's 12:00 p.m. He starts to dial a number and thought he shouldn't. He walks to the kitchen and passes a photo of the band, and begin to look at the picture all dreamy like touching Pete's picture as if he's making love to it. -Not too deep- but as if he has feelings for him.)

*Fade Out*
***SWITCH*** 

Like:

I can't believe this is happening. I need to run by the school, I need to collect my thoughts, gather my songs, warm up my voice, clear my mind and arrange my life.

Devin:

Dad!

Like:

Yes son.

Devin:

Can I come with you tonight?

Like:

(Gets himself together.) Well, son it seems as though you will be coming with me tonight. Wait! You can't...What am I doing? I'm the leader of the band the man with the plans and my wife has left me on one of the most important nights of my life.

Devin:

Dad did you say mommy was gone?

Like:

No Devin. She's gone to your auntie's to catch her breath.

Devin:

I did that last night.

Like:
(Not listening.)

Devin:
I did that last night when mom said she had to catch her breath. I asked how do you catch your breath? (Demonstrating.) And she did like this (Inhales very fast and exhales slowly) so I told her to take her time.

Like:
Yes son you are right she should take her time. (He himself inhales and exhales. And squeezes the child lovingly).

*Fade Out*
*(Eeshun and Cindy have come up on the school's pool. They read the sign
and hesitate on going in. They think it over and goes in anyway.)*

Cindy:
Why did we come in here? You know the last time I was in here Rodney Brown was playing peeping Tom.

Eeshun:
I know, but you have to admit it was pretty funny though.

Cindy:
Yeah, we can say that now.

***(TIME SWITCH 1978)***

(Both of the girls' backs are turned towards the camera. The camera pans up from Cindy's legs and Eeshun is on the bench. Both are already dressed in their swimsuits and they are putting lotion on their bodies. The camera spots Rodney Brown looking at them through a hole in the wall. Then it cuts to them at the pool site learning rescue maneuvers.)

Rodney Brown:
Hey Cindy Charlatan I wish I was that lotion going across your knees, up your thighs, across your stomach and up to your bre...

Like:
(Walks up to Rodney Brown) Bite me! (Pushes the crap out of him into the pool and smacks or shakes hands with Day Beens, but didn't look back at Cindy.)

Eeshun:
(Looks at Cindy, she knows Cindy is peeved off.) Don't worry about him Cindy he's just showing off.

Cindy:
(Looking at Like with the Goo-Goo eyes, but he's not looking at her.) I know...

*(TIME SWITCH 1999)*

Eeshun:
But we did look good though,

Girls:
(Laughs)

Cindy:
Yeah we did.

*Fade Out*
*(Sometimes we have to paint pictures to help others see.)*

Trish:
(In studio listening to a group.) Cut, Cut, Cut! Listen you guys I need some feelings. Wait I know everyone says that...Think as if someone has broken into your home where you and your only sister has grew up in with one red boxer, both parents, fudge brownies and pecan pies every Sunday. When they broke in they not only stole the television, but they took your only sister for their own pleasures. You really miss your sister and you know that she's out there somewhere so you wrote this song for her.

Everyone:
(Looks at her as if she has just open up a closed wound.)

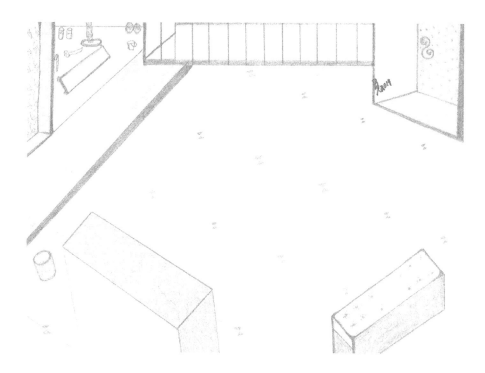

Trish:

Okay people maybe not that deep. (Phone rings.) I want feelings, I want true feelings. Okay? (On phone.) Hello... Hi Charles. Thanks for calling. Would you like to go to the club tonight? No not really. Well would you think about it? Oh okay...Well call me back if you change your mind. Peace. (Flops back in to her chair.) Take ten.

*Be patient it will be over soon.*

Bece:

(Checks his watch.) How's it coming guys?

Woody:

It's looking pretty good from here. (He's at the back with the trunk up, body halfway in attaching the speakers.)

Bece:

Well you should know. You have been through this whole car from front to back.

Beep:

You mean that figuratively or literally?

Bece:
You figure it out English major.

Woody:
You've been pretty impatient since you've been back.

Bece:
My mom is going to kill me...

Beep:
Momma's boy.

Bece:
It's not like that... You wouldn't understand.

Woody:
It's okay Bece. It's almost done. Shut up Beep. You are always putting your foot in your mouth.

Beep:
Yo man I'm chilled.

Boys:
(Continue to work diligently.)

*Fade Out*

*Before you make any decisions think it over with yourself, first.*

Pete Rosalyn:
(In car thinking out loud.)
I'm tired of being the errand boy. He's the youngest, he needs to learn the ropes around here. He needs some muscles, he's so frail. His dad must be on the slim side. I'm the butt of all jokes... Well they won't be laughing tonight. What am I talking about, this is my job, this is how I eat and sleep. I couldn't even find a decent band to play with four months ago. So whom am I fooling? I will have to do and take whatever I can get right now.

*Fade Out*

(At the restaurant: Lady C. is looking in on the banquet.
Everyone is eating, laughing, and praising the food.)

Waitress:

Lady don't stand out here and watch him at his dirty work.

Lady:

Why do people hate to see other people doing well?

Waitress:

They want everything for themselves. This world is so large that we should be able to breath without someone telling us "You're taking in all the oxygen."

Lady:

Ha, Ha, Ha don't quit your day job.

Waitress:

Maybe that wasn't exactly what I was trying to say.

Lady:

I'm just kidding. I know exactly what you are trying to say.

Waitress:

(Looking out at the guests) They are talking about you Lady, but they don't know it's you whom they're complementing.

Lady:

Well I want them to know it's me. I've been doing this line of work for over thirty years now. When I came here I was the first black ever to work here in the kitchen, as a cook, yeah but I was doing something I like.

**\*(TIME SWITCH 1963)\***

Mr. Larue:
(In kitchen.) I would like for you to meet our new short order cook. What is your name girl?

Lady:
(Soft spoken)
Lady Charlatan.

Mr. Larue:
Speak up girl so they can hear you…

Lady:
(A little louder)
Lady C…

Mr. Larue:
I'll give you the quick orientation (He gives her a pencil and pad.) Write things down so you won't forget them because I am not going over it again.

Lady:
(Looks at pencil and pad.)…That's okay I have an excellent memory. (She tries to give it back to him, but he refuses them nasty politely. She places the items into her pocket.)

Mr. Larue:
(He walks around the kitchen.) Over here is where we keep the fresh vegetables. We try to use everything. If the lettuce is brown, chop the brown stuff off. If the right side of the tomato is spoiled chop it off and use the rest of it, and so on. Do not throw away whole vegetables. There is always a part you can use. (Lady is shocked, but she is not showing it because this is her first job at an all white establishment. I guess she gets the impression that this is how they do.) Over here we keep the meats and we take the same approach with everything around here. Silverware is here, pots here, napkins, dollies, and on, and on, and on… Any questions ask one of your peers. (Camera pans across all the black faces in the kitchen. The blacks are kitchen hands they are never seen. White boys and girls are waiters and waitresses. The white cooks are entitled as Culinary Art Chefs. So she knew exactly what he meant. He walks off and Lady is looking on.)

# *-SWITCH 1999-*

Lady:
(Time has changed.) I guess some things never change. (Then she notices that the waitress isn't there anymore.)

Like:
(We see him cleaning and picking-up around the house. Devin is in his room. Like decides to use the phone.)
 Hi Ginnie, is Melody there? Well have you seen or heard from her? Well, thanks okay… but that sounds like her in the background. No, No that isn't her. Well, if you do hear from her or even see her, will you tell her kindly that she can take all the time she would like. We will be right here.

Devin:
Dad, dad is that mommy on the phone, tell her don't forget that this is the night we watch the cartoon movie of the week.

Like:
No son, this isn't your mom, but I will keep that in mind. All right? (Back on phone.) "G" I'll talk to you later. (She hangs up and it cuts to the two women in Auntie Ginni's house.)

Devin:
(Back at Like's house.) That was auntie Ginni? You said that mom was at auntie Ginni's house.

Like:
Well son it doesn't seems as though she's made it over there yet. She might be running some errands first. (He's looking very uncertain of that.)

Devin:
Dad are you all right? (Like nods.) It's spaghetti night, mom makes the best spaghetti.

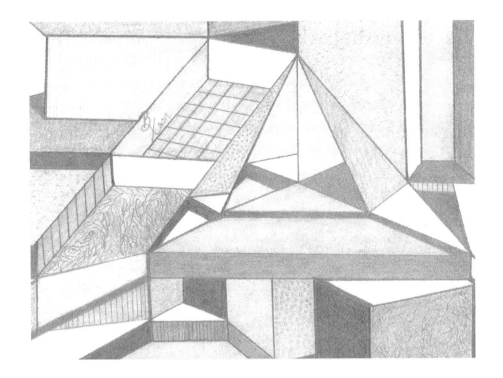

Like:
I don't think we'll be having spaghetti tonight.

Devin:
Why?

Like:
Because mommy isn't here to make it.

Devin:
Why?

Like:
She stepped out.

Devin:
Why?

Like:
Listen Devin I'll stop and get you some hot burgers and fries. This will be a good time for a change.

Devin:
Why?

Like:
Because we haven't had a father and son day since I've known when. So we'll make the best out of it. (Devin was about to speak, and Like puts his finger up to Devin's lips.) And please son no more questions right now. I can't think this fast.

Devin:
Why?

*Unsolved Mysteries*

Day:
Why are there so many delays Ms.?

Receptionist:
Sir, we are really not allowed to tell any passengers what's going on today.

Day:
It has to be major since planes have landed and you all are not allowing any to go up.

Receptionist:
It is sir. We apologize for any inconveniences.

Day:
I have a gig in Atlanta tonight will I be able to make it today?

Receptionist:
We will get you there today, but I can't state any specific times for you sir.

Day:
(Whisper, politely.) Is there any way I could get a train ticket for an exchange of a plane ticket?

Receptionist:
I do believe you can sir. I'll get on it right now.

Day:
Thanks.

## *-SWITCH-*

Eeshun:
Since we are here we should go and see the old Theatre.

Cindy:
What I can't believe you want to go there after falling down those stairs at the last big production. (With a laugh.)

Eeshun:
That is not funny. My ankle is still messed up from that fall. (They both look down at the ankle.)

Eeshun:
(Continue.) What are you looking at you didn't even see the fall.

### *(TIME SWITCH. 1979 School play written by Cindy. "TuFF" In school theatre.)*

Cindy:
Look, I know that at some crossroads it seem as though there just isn't enough choices, but really there's always a choice.

Like:
Well I don't know which one to choose.

Cindy:
Choose the one that makes you happy.

Like:
What makes me happy is something that might hurt a lot of people.

Cindy:

Well as my mom always said, "Make the most positive decision with the less negative outcome."

Like:

(He looks her deep into her eyes, right then Eeshun starts to fall down the stairs. They try not to look into the audience, but they do.) You make a lot of sense. (Very close to each other as to kiss, but didn't and he smiles genuinely. Eeshun lands at the bottom of the stairs by a pair of shoes.)

***(TIME SWITCH BACK 1999.)***

Eeshun:

You should have just kissed him.

Cindy:

It wasn't written like that.

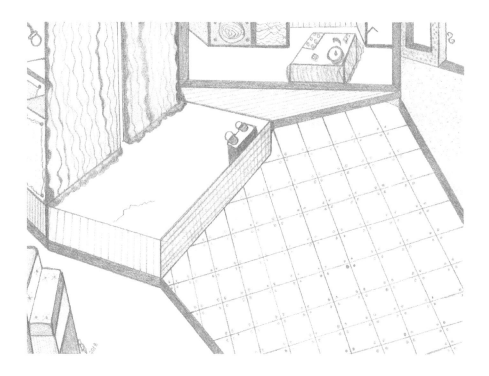

Eeshun:

See we shouldn't have started thinking about them.

Cindy:
It's all these different rooms that keep conjuring up all these mixed feelings.

Eeshun:
Is that good or bad?

Cindy:
It's bad. It all happen (20) twenty years ago. Dah!

Eeshun:
Yeap, but they were the good times.

Cindy:
Yeap, you can say that again.

Eeshun:
What does that mean? (Knowing that she knows something.)-?-

Cindy:
I know about you and Mr. Day Beens (Benz).

Eeshun:
(Slightly shocked.) You know what?

*-SWITCH-*

Waitress:
The luncheon is coming to a closure.

Lady:
And what does that mean?

Waitress:
There's still hope that Mr. Larue will change his mind.

Lady:

It's okay even if he doesn't.

Waitress:
Lady, how can you say that?

Lady:
Easily. I think I intimidate Mr. Larue. He knows literally that I make this business go around and around... As I look around the kitchen all his well- known chefs are gone and I'm the last one standing. He actually changed the title of the position once he noticed he didn't have anyone else left to promote but me. He
would never let anybody know that it's me doing all the cooking.

Waitress:
Look, Lady I believe that there's always a good chance that someone can change for the better and it still can happen today.

V.O Waitress:
Do I even believe It myself?

*-Fade Out-*

*On the phone again?*

Trish:
Hey I'm feeling better already Mr. Clearly. I know the ideal I have in my head and I believe it can work with this group. I spoke with the leader of the band and he speaks as if he has his head on straight too. I want the sound track to go as smooth as a baby's bottom. I want our listeners to see the movie in their heads everytime they hear a song off the sound track. Let the music tell the story. I think as soon as Cindy Chocolate gets off this yearly hiatus of hers she'll agree thoroughly. I don't know why every time around this time of the year she goes into this shell. Well, it's okay because she always come back ready to work. Yes Mr. Clearly I'll keep my head clear, my ears open, and my eyes on the prize.

***-SWITCH-***

Pete Rosalyn:

I can't believe this. This traffic reminds me of the '96 Olympics. I got to use the bathroom and I'm almost on "E". (Cell phone rings.) Hello, Tiggs is that you? What's taking me so long? The traffic is horrendous out here. What is going on? This whole day seems as though something has gone wrong. It feels like a new beginning or the end of something; I can't really tell.

### *-SWITCH-*

*On the phone too.*

Tiggs:

Pete, there's something I'd like to say to you and please don't interrupt me. I'm crazy about you and I can't shake it. I try to keep it under wraps, but it gets so hard sometimes… Sometimes I want to hold you so tight, but I can't. Well I thought you should know how I feel about you.

*-Car Scene-*

Pete:

What you're expressing your feelings? I told you something is going on today.

*It's just getting started.*

Bece:

I'm going to get something to drink, would you all care for anything?

Woody:

I want some cookies.

Beep:

I'll take a Yahoo.

Bece:

(Holds out his hand.) I was going to treat y'all right, but since it's taking y'all so long I'll wait until the job is done and tip y'all then. But for right now you're on your own. Money Please? (With hand out.)

Boys:
Well, Thank you.

### *-SWITCH-*

Like:
(Like and Devin just got finish eating a big junk food meal. Like not doing so bad for his son's sake. This situation is still on his mind, but he's spending quality time with his son. So it's not so bad.) Devin, don't tell your mother about the things we ate today.

Devin:
That was fun! I know not to put my foot in my mouth.

Like:
How do you know that cliche?

Devin:
I heard you tell one of the band members that.

Like:
Oh, that was Big Guss.

Devin:
(Laughs) Yeap, that's him dad he's a funny man.

Like:
Who talks a little too much and he… (Looks at Devin. Both of them together.)

Like/Devin:
Always put his foot in his mouth .

Like:
Like's father, Like's son... (Pause.) You know how I always say stay in school and get your education? Well, we are going to my old school to pick up some items for the gig tonight.

Devin:
Dad, I get to see where you got your education?

Like:
Yes, you do son. (He turns on the radio.)

*Fade Out*

**\*-SWITCH-\***

Eeshun:
(They are walking into the music room and Cindy turns on the radio.) What do you know about Day and I ?

Cindy:
Nothing.

Eeshun:
Yes you do Cindy.

Cindy:
You called me Cindy. It must be something to know.

Eeshun:
(As if she's scolding Cindy pointing her finger.) What do you know C-C?

Cindy:
Nothing, is there something to know?

Eeshun:
You tell me.

Cindy:
You tell me.

Radio Announcer:
We interrupt your broadcasting to inform the world that John F. Kennedy Jr. plane went down last night over Martha's Vineyard. He, his wife and his wife's sister were on their way to John- John's cousin Rory's wedding. They haven't found any wreckage so stay tuned and we'll keep you posted.

Cindy:
No, Oh No, it's happening again.

Eeshun:
What is happening again?

Cindy:
This morning I had this horrible dream and I thought it was just because it was Bart's anniversary.

Eeshun:
I didn't even put two and two together. I don't even know what two things I'm talking about.

Cindy:
(Reenacting the dream.)
I dreamt I was on a plane and I had to go to the bathroom. I was in the front of the plane so I had to walk all the way to the back. Well I walked down the aisle and it kept getting longer and longer so I started to look from side to side at the passengers. I saw Bart, Pasty Cline, Buddy Holly and I was doing fine because I thought I was going to make it to the back (We see Bart at the back with two empty seats on the side of him.) where Bart was. Then I looked to the side one more time and I saw John F. Kennedy Jr. sitting there with two women and they were chatting. So I tried to stop and talk and he just turned to looked at me and said:

John Jr.:
It's not your turn. Then I woke up.

Eeshun:

Oh, my goodness C-C, You didn't say anything all day. I almost didn't remember that today is Bart's anniversary.

Cindy:

I've been working on my slump.

Eeshun:

That's not a slump.

Cindy:

Not negatively, it's just not healthy to go through it every year.

Eeshun:

You can go through it as long as it takes you to get over it.
And you might not ever get over it, but you will be able to get through it.

Cindy:

Thanks Eeshun…(Pause) My heart goes out to their families.

### *-SWITCH-*

Devin:

Dad did you hear that?

Like:

Yes I did son. How do you know about John F. Kennedy Jr.?

Devin:

From my school. We had to do a small report on people who are making a difference in 1999.

Like:

(Paused because he didn't help.) Hmmm, I guess your mom helped you with that one?

Devin:

Yes, sir.

Like:
Well, next time I'll help also. We all need to be informed about the people who are making a difference in the world, and not just for their sake.

Devin:
Yep, dad he did a lot for the girls and boys club too.

Like:
Well, I'm quite sure all his goodness will not go unnoticed. I hope everything is okay, but if not they were all surrounded by love ones.

Devin:
I love you dad.

Like:
I love you too son...and your mom.

## *-SWITCH-*

*Don't rush me. I'll be there in a minute.*

*(We pan over the restaurant and everyone is wrapping up the day, cheerfully.

Then we hear a couple of dishes break in the kitchen. We pan to Mr. Larue's face expression and he's looking as if he's lost another $20.00. Then he walks into the kitchen.)*

Mr. Larue:
(Everyone is quiet looking at the t.v.) What is going on in here?

Helper:
John F. Kennedy Jr.'s plane went down last night with him, his wife and his wife's sister on board.

Mr. Larue:
Well, let's not stop working shall we…?

Lady:
I think we should have a moment of silence for the family.

Mr. Larue:
We don't have time for that kind of thing around here.

Waiter:
I think we should Mr. Larue.

> (As they discuss the issue at hand, a helper leaves the kitchen out the back where the guests are seated. He finds one of the guest who so happens to be a well known Reverend around the community, and politely whispered in his ear what he just heard on the television.)

Reverend James Holt:
(In plain clothing.) I've just been informed that John F. Kennedy Jr.'s plane went down last night with him, his wife and his sister-in- law on board. So I would like to have a prayer for the family. Can we please gather together for a moment of unity? Stand everyone (Looks at helper) please call all the workers in, the more we have to come together the better we are heard.

Helper:
(Enter kitchen.) There's a Reverend out here and he wants everyone to come together and have one big prayer for the Kennedy-Bessette's family.

> (Larue and Lady look at each other. Lady looks as if to say that is the humane thing to do. And Mr. Larue's face is tight.)

### *-SWITCH-*

> *(Moving, music scene.)
> We see Bece going up the stairs.
> *We see Cindy and Eeshun walking down the hall.
> *We see Like and Devin getting out of the car. They are parked pretty close to Eeshun and Cindy.*

**\*Bece is going up the stairs at one end of the hall, at the same time his mom is walking down the hall and we see Like and Devin walking into the building.\***

\*(We want to show that people and situations can be so close yet too far away)\*.

### \*-SWITCH-\*

\*(Everyone comes out of the kitchen. Larue and Lady are the last ones to walk out.)\*

Reverend James Holt:
As we come together in this room, we should think about the growth of the world. (As the Rev. speaks they start to hold hands, some hesitates, but there's a lot of them who join hands without any problems. Lady sees the Reverend hand extra extended out to hers as welcoming as any other hand. Then he speaks.) Come, (Looking at Lady.) lets join together for a true blessing to the Kennedy's and the Bessette's.

Lady:
(Holds his hand.) Thank you.

Reverend James Holt:

Lord as we set here today and enjoyed this wonderful meal you were out working on something else. Life never comes with an instruction manual and a end of the day planner, so we try to do the right things day by day until you call upon us. We don't know if you called upon the Kennedy-Bessette family or not, but if so you should see that they are ready for you. We might not be ready for them to leave, but it's in your hands and those are the best hands to be in; in these days and times...

I would like to bless the cook who prepared this meal that brought us all together... (Lady cuts him off politely.)

Lady:

You are welcome. Lord thank you for blessing me with loving hands to prepare such a wonderful meal. And Lord please keep my heart, mind, and belly filled with all your gracious blessings. Thank you.

Reverend James Holt:

(Pause slightly, looks at Lady and continues.) Well Lord bless this group, may we never forget this day and the way we all joined together and prayed. Everyone look up, but keep on holding hands so you can remember the people around you. Amen. (The circle stays bonded and they all look at each other a little longer. There are all types of people standing together. Then they drop hands.)

### *-SWITCH-*

(We now see Cindy and Eeshun in the mechanic shop. We see Like and Devin in the chorus and band room, and Bece is at the store.)

*The boys are still working on the car.*

Cindy:

Excuse me (They didn't hear her. They just finished listening to the radio too.) Excuse me do you all know Bece Jones? That's his car you're working on.

Woody:

(Turns around with all smiles because he knows right away who she is.) Yes ma'am we know Bece Jones.

Beep:
Are you Mrs. Cindy Chocolate?

Girls:
Yes. (They look at each other then Cindy speaks.)

Cindy:
Yes I am. We're looking for Bece he has my car keys. Are you almost finished with his car?

Boys:
Yes ma' am.

Beep:
Is Bece your son?

Cindy:
Yes he is.

Beep:
I always thought he was kidding.

Woody:
I told you he wasn't.

Beep:
Mrs. Jones we will have his car done in a jiffy.

Cindy:
Where is he?

Boys:
At the store.

Woody:

He should be back shortly. (We see Like and Devin passing the outside window going towards the band room.)

Cindy:

Just tell him I came by, but to hold on to my keys and get my car back in one piece. Mrs. Cindy Chocolate may I have your autograph?

Cindy:

Sure, where would you like it?

Beep:

(Gives this eye as to say something nasty and Woody smacks him on the head.) In my hand so I can look at it all day.

Woody:

Me too. (Cindy begins to write on the guys' hands.)

Eeshun:

Okay you two that's enough of the private section with Cindy Chocolate. Next time you'll have to pay. Now get back to work, and it shouldn't take you all day either.

Boys:

(Stands at attention and salutes the women.) Yes ma'am.

Girls:

(They laugh and exit the room.)

Eeshun:

Well let's get going they seem as though they have everything under control.

Cindy:

Girl yes I can't take anymore of this reminiscing.

Eeshun:
It was fun though.

Cindy:
Yep it was fun though. (They walk the opposite direction of Like and Devin, but they do hear a kids' laughter and look back in that direction.) It sounds like we're not the only ones having fun either. (They keep on walking.)

*-SWITCH-*

Trish:
(Startled at Mr. David Clearly presence.) Mr. Clearly what are you doing here?

David Clearly:
I had to get away. I was getting too emotional over the Kennedy's. So I thought I'd come to the studio and be productive...So are you still going to the concert tonight?

Trish:
Yes sir. I just got this new look on things after hearing the report too. I need to do as much as I can. Anything can happen at any given time and when it does I want people to say Dang that girl was always doing something.

David Clearly:
Well, what are you doing here still talking to me? You need to be out doing some thing.

(David starts to walk around the studio admiring the photos on the walls and stares at the one with this little old woman on it with him.)

Trish:
You miss her don't you Mr. Clearly?

David Clearly:
My mom always said that our name fits me because she could see straight through me. (Touching the picture.) Yes I miss her, she is a wonderful mother.

Trish:
It's okay Mr. Clearly I'm quite sure she misses you too…Maybe you can go and see her after the rush. (Getting ready to walk out and thinks twice.) Would you like to come with me tonight and relax your mind a little? They say a lot of pretty women are there.

David Clearly:
(Shakes his head.) I'll go.

Trish:
Good I'll pick you up at 9 o'clock okay Mr. Clearly.

David Clearly:
Ms. Spears call me David tonight.

Trish:
And Mr. David call me Trish okay. (Both smile.)

### *-SWITCH-*

Like:
(They are finish-packing things for the gig. Stands, microphones, lights, drum sticks, disco globe, etc ...) Son will you open the door please?

Devin:
(Walks over to the door to open it.)

Like:
(Is trying to carry everything in one trip. As soon as he gets into the hallway, he drops everything. He and Devin are both bent down trying to pick up the items. Then they see a pair of shoes.)

Bece:
May I help you guys?

Like:
Sure.

Bece:
Y'all not robbing my school are you?

Like:
No. I use to go here twenty years ago and I still have permission to use the equipment if need be. (Shows keys to Bece.) See I have my own keys too.

Bece:
Well hi, Im Bece Jones.

Like:
I'm Like Waters and my son Devin.

Devin:
Hello, you're in high school? I can't wait to get into high school. I'll be able to drive and my folks can't tell me what to do.

Bece:
You were sounding pretty good until you got to that last one. Your parents will always be able to tell you what to do. Believe me parents have the best experiences. I know my mom is still telling me about hers. (By this time everything is picked up and they are walking to the car.)

Like:
Why thanks a lot Bece.

Bece:
No, problems Mr. Waters.

Devin:
Will I see you again Bece? I need a big guy like you to show me the ropes.

Like:
You got me to show you the ropes, son.

Devin:
Dad you're too old, I need someone young like me.

Bece:
Nooo, Devin I'm not trying to go back to your age, but I know what you mean. Here take my number and call me sometimes. I'll be a big brother to you.

Devin:
Dad did you hear that? I got myself a big brother. (Repeat optional.)

Like and Bece:
(Shake hands.)

Like:
Thank your parents, for raising such a nice son.

## *-SWITCH-*

(At the restaurant everyone is leaving the circle mingling, and Lady was on her way to the back when the Reverend stopped her.)

Rev. James Holt:
Excuse me Miss I assume that was you who prepare that wonderful meal? I told my wife that someone really knows how to make a Cornish hen like my mother does.

Lady:
Yes sir that is I, and I got the recipe from my mother.

Rev. James Holt:
Listen, I'm having a Unity Banquet Ball and I would love for you to be the guest chef or shall I ask you what would you like for me to call you?

Lady:
Lady, just call me Lady C. And for my cooking I would like to be properly appreciated for my work. (Not going to let anyone get over anymore.) I'm quite sure you know how to conduct business Mr. Reverend James Holt?

Rev. James Holt:
(Feeling the "I'm not trusting you demeanor". So he's reassuring her.) Yes, I'm sure the Lord will conduct business quite nicely, he lead us to meet didn't he? (By this time Larue has moved into the picture.)

Lady:
(Softens up a little now.) Thank you Rev. I would love to. I don't mean to be defensive, I'm just tired of being ripped off in my line of work. (Looks up at Mr. Larue.)

Rev. James Holt:
Believe me we might not be from the same line of work, but I do know about getting ripped off. The Lord will repay you generously just be patient my dear Lady.

Lady:

Patience is all I have.

## *-SWITCH-*

*(Eeshun and Cindy are in the car almost home.)*

Cindy:

Girl this has been an interesting day. Maybe we needed that stroll down memory lane to bring back some of our youth. (Eeshun gives no response.) What's wrong "E"?

Eeshun:

I wish we didn't do so much reminiscing now I can't stop thinking about Day. I should have gone with him to LA. Just to see how it would have been, but I was too scared.

Cindy:

It's okay to be scared.

Eeshun:

That's easy for you to say. You went ahead and got married had a child and have a wonderful career now.

Cindy:

(Not getting the point.)
You have accomplished some many things too Eeshun. You have a million dollars a year plus more grossing company, you have your health and you drive this phat car.

Eeshun:

I know, But I don't have a steady man nor my own family to teach morals and values to.

Cindy:

It's not too late Eeshun. You're just a little behind the rest of us. Keep hope alive.

Eeshun:

(Smiles.) Okay.

Cindy:
You really did like Day didn't you?

Eeshun:
Yes, but we were just as different as night and day.

Cindy:
That doesn't mean it couldn't have worked.

Eeshun:
I was scared, I was going to run him away with my flyaway thoughts and decisions. Now, that looks like something I will never find out.

Cindy:
We will find him Eeshun.

Eeshun:
Don't worry about it "C" he might not even remember me.

Cindy:
Who can forget Eeshun Denise Wells?

Eeshun:
Day no middle name Beens. (Benz.)

Cindy:
Cheer up… I'll see you at 9 o'clock, we're going to have fun tonight okay.

Eeshun:
All right. 9: o'clock, bye.

Cindy:
Bye.

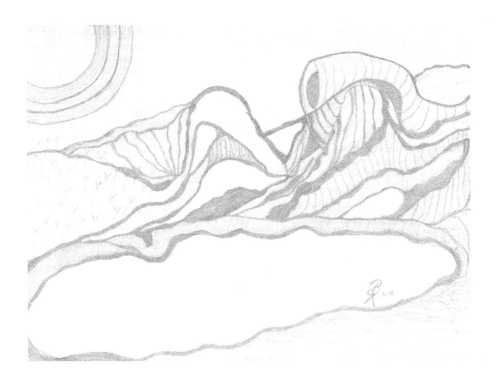

### *-SWITCH-*

(Day Beens is on a train riding through open fields of wide land enjoying every peaceful moment of silent time to himself. This is a tricky scene; I'm still trying to figure out how I will pull this one off myself. So enjoy the ride. First, he's awake daydreaming, then he snaps out of that and actually goes to sleep the next round.)

Day:
(Staring out of the window and falls deep into his thoughts.)

Momma Day:
Day, I know it's hard for you to adjust to this way of living.

Day:
Why are we always moving?

Momma Day:
You know your father goes wherever the wind sends him.

Day:
It's the band isn't it?

Momma Day:
Yep, if the city isn't treating them well, they have to keep on moving.

Day:
Why do you put up with him mom?

Momma Day:
People always said that it was hard to love a musician. When I see your father holding that guitar you can see it all in his body language that he is sitting on top of the world. You can tell he has a lot of love in him. He sways side to side, head slightly dropped and his eyes are closed, but his mind, heart, body, and soul is wide open for the world to see and hear. Then he opens his eyes and he see that he's still right here.

Day:
So mom what are you saying?

Momma Day:
I knew for a long time that there wasn't too much that could come between him and that guitar, but when we met face to face, he held me so tight yet gentle and looked me dead in my eyes I knew I was his best guitar yet for the plucking.

Day:
Eew, mom you're talking nasty.

Momma Day:
(Laughs.) Just remember he's a good man son and I believe you can handle this way of life.

### *BACK TO REALITY*

Day:
She just didn't tell me it would be so lonely down this road. (Now Day falls asleep, and now it's all about Eeshun )

Eeshun:
I don't know if I can go with you Day. You know what you want.

Day:
I really don't know what I want. I just know that you are about the most stable thing in my life.

Eeshun:
We haven't even gotten a title for our rendezvous.

Day:
That's you who are scared to commit.

Eeshun:
I'm just so scared that...

Day:
(Cuts her off.)
That's all we talk about is you being so scared. You need to stop being scared Eeshun that will only hold you back. Maybe there isn't anything left for us to talk about. (He walks off.)

Eeshun:
(Low undertone.) I'm just scared to love you Day.

*(Day awakens)*

Day:
(With a startled look.) She said something didn't she?

**\*-SWITCH-\***

*(Bece is now back in the building and he is where his boys are.)*

Beep:
Bece I saw your mom and dude she is fine as hell.

Bece:
Beep don't talk about my mom like that. When did you see her?

Woody:
She just left like 15 minutes ago.

Bece:
You are kidding right?

Boys:
Nope.

Bece:
Did she seem upset?

Woody:
Nope, she just said to bring her car back in one piece.

Beep:
We are almost finish with putting things back in their proper places.

Bece:
I knew you had some correct grammar in that head of yours somewhere.

Beep:
Anything to ride back with you to drop your mom's car off.

Woody:
I'm riding too.

Bece:
I knew it, you guys are using me to see my mom.

Boys:
What are friends for?

## *-SWITCH-*

(The answer machine at Like's and Devin's house.)

Melody:

Honey it's me. I called to check on you and Devin. I hope everything is going fine. Maybe I was talking out of my head the first time I called. I just have so much on my mind that I needed some time to think. I do miss you and Devin. I'm still catching my breath, but I do believe we can still breathe together as one big happy family. I want you to know that I'm not a doormat, waitress, chauffeur, housekeeper and love slave. I'm your wife the love slave ain't so bad, and I'm Devin's mother and I want you guys to realize it's not easy to be me in a house where I'm doing all the work. I lose sight on who I am... Maybe I said too much. (Beep)!

**\*(We now see a picture by the phone of Like's mom and a black man.)\***

## *-SWITCH-*

*Note where everybody is at this point.
*Bece still at school with boys and car. *Cindy just been dropped off, be ready at 9:pm. *Eeshun is in car driving. *Day is on train. *Like and Devin are leaving the school. *Lady and Larue are at the restaurant. *Tiggs is at home. *Pete is still at the airport. *Trish and Mr. Clearly are coming to the concert.*

*(At Tiggs house. We see him getting out of the shower. Bathroom mirror is fogged up. He dries off his face then wipe clear the mirror, he stares at it a moment (dreamy like) time switch.* Note when it happens it's not as noticeable as the other time changes. The person, and place doesn't change just the time.* Shower is running again we see a figure in the shower.)*

Girl:
So what do you think I should do?

Tiggs:
(Startled.) Are you talking to me?

Girl:
Who else would I be talking to?

Tiggs:
Do what you feel is right.

Girl:
I think working and playing my drums is right, but it doesn't seems as though both of them are going to work out together.

Tiggs:
Yes it will work out.

Girl:
How?

Tiggs:
We will think of something.

Girl:
Are you sure?

Tiggs:
I'm never too sure about anything, but I feel pretty positive about this.

Girl:
Well, good that's what I want to hear.

Tiggs:
(Walking over to the shower about to open it.) Well good I got something you might want to see too. (Time has changed slowly. He opens the door and no one is in there.) Snap (Disappointed) I need to stop this daydreaming.

## *-SWITCH-*

Pete:
Excuse me, the plane I was waiting for has landed already, but I don't see the person I was waiting for.

Receptionist:
Yes, and...

Pete:
And I want to know could you tell me if they took another flight or route period?

Receptionist:

Yes, I could check to see if they are on another flight, but there's no way of knowing if they take another route.

Pete:
Well good could you check it out please?

Receptionist:
Yes, sir.

Pete :
Thanks.

## *-SWITCH-*

Larue:
Lady, Lady may I have a word with you?

Lady:
(With her stern looks and ways shining though.) Yes.

Larue:
I know that I'm not the easiest person to deal with, and I know that I can be down right rude at times.

Lady:
Most of the time.

Larue:
I know.

Lady:
What's your point Mr. Larue?

Larue:
You are really good at what you do.

Lady:
So I am now!?

Larue:
Yes, you are.

Lady:
So what took you so long to notice that? And why are you bringing it up now?

Larue:
All the other ones have left me and you are the last man standing.

Lady:
No, I'm a Lady.

Larue:
Yes, the last Lady standing, and I can feel the leaving itch coming on.

Lady:
Is that right?

Larue:
Yes, Lady and I'm not ready for you to leave.

Lady:
Is it because I'm the last Lady standing or because I'm Damn good at what I do? I usually don't curse, so you better answer with some truth.

Larue:
(Silence)

Lady:
I knew it. (She begins to walk off.) I knew it.

Larue:

No, wait Lady. I'm always losing something or someone so I turned myself into someone, who's hard and controlling, so I wouldn't have time to find, keep, share, or even hold on to someone, anyone or anything.

Lady:
Well it worked.

Larue:
But not with you. You stayed, you hung on in there, you learned the ropes and you operate and run the back like a pro. I couldn't figure out why my workers wasn't listening to me anymore… It was you.

Lady:
I was doing my job Mr. Larue.

Larue:
And you do your job well.

Lady:
Can you say that again?

Larue:
You do your job well.

*(Time period switch. 1948)*

*Lady is at a chalkboard as a young girl, Little Lady, with 3 other kids doing word problems. The kids finished their problems and Lady stands alone.*

Lady's Teacher:
Lady, can you do that word problem on the board? You've been up there for five minutes, everyone else has read and solved their problems and you are standing up there like an empty wagon.

Kids:
(Laughs.)

Lady:
I am not an empty wagon.

One Kid:
She can't read.

Kids:
(Laughs.)

Teacher:
Calm down class, calm down. Lady are you having difficulties reading the word problem?

Lady:
Yes, ma'am.

Teacher:
I'm glad you brought that to my attention. I'll read it out loud to you and you write down the problem to solve it. We will spend more time on your reading one on one during recess.

Lady:
(Completes the word problem without any problems and got the answer right.)

*(Time Switch back to 1999)*

Lady:
That's all you have to do is take the time to get to know someone because you never know what roads lead them here. I am not an empty wagon and you will not treat me like one anymore and people will not get the last laugh off me unless I've told a funny joke. That's the only way I'm not walking out of these doors.

Larue:
Yes, ma'am … Well. I'm not letting you go. Lady you are truly a Lady and I will always respect you for that. So would you like the rest of the week off with a raise?

Lady:
Yes, I would thank you.

## *-SWITCH-*

*(Story line)*
*Everyone's problem is starting to come together. Now we need
to start drawing a conclusion. Things are taking form.)*

*We still love to talk to our mothers everyday and believe
me they don't want it no other way.*

Cindy:
(On phone at home.)
Mom, call me when you get in. I want to know how your banquet went today. And just in case you're wondering, yes I'm still going out tonight. (She hangs up.)

## *-TIME SWITCH 1979-*

Cindy:
Mom have you seen my black heels?

Lady:
(Opens door.) You are putting on heels?

Cindy:
Yes, ma'am why you ask?

Lady:
This must be a really nice guy to make you want to wear a pair of heels.

Cindy:
They are black heels, momma.

Lady:
Well excuse me, he haven't gotten you out of black yet so he must not be too special.

Cindy:
Mom, I don't even think he knows that I exist.

Lady:

Who can miss you Cindy? You are a wonderful girl, smart, cute and independent.

Cindy:

Yep, but I think that does more damage than help.

Lady:

Never. If it was any other way they'll still find something to complain about. So enjoy what you have, make the best out of what you do, and never move too fast.

Cindy:

Why thank you mom… So do you think this black is too much?

Lady:

For tonight, it is...

### *-SWITCH 1999-*

Cindy:
(Looking into mirror.)
I feel like a little girl , I'm too tickled pink.

-*End of scene-*

-*( Back with boys Getting things together with a music monologue. Bece, and Beep are getting into Bece's car and Woody is driving Cindy's car. Trish is at the studio listening to an excellent group ,that's who song we hear throughout the scenes.

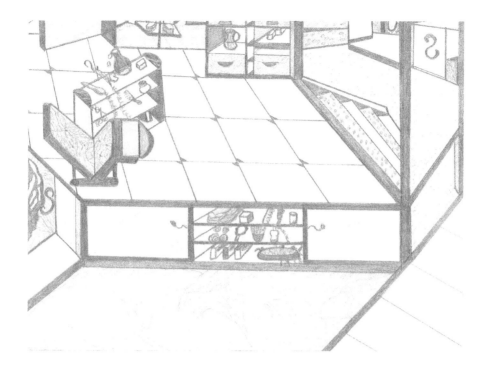

Eeshun is driving by her business. She slows down and look at all the cars in the parking lot. She had to think about all the things she has accomplished and the roads she traveled to get here. Then she starts to drive away because she's really not ready to face up to the pain she has endured to get where she is today.

We see Tiggs all dressed and looking nice. We see Mr. Clearly looking around at his house, but really focusing on this one picture of him and a white lady on it. Like and Devin are heading back into the house. The same as Like's Picture.*

Devin:
(He sees the phone message button is lit up.) Mom called dad, mom called.

Like:
Calm down Devin that might not be her.

Devin:
I have this feeling that it is her.

Like:
(Listen to the message. Privately.) Well, son it sounds as though she's going to be fine.

Devin:

I'ma go clean up my bathroom and bedroom so mom won't have to do it. Whatcha going to do dad?

Like:

(Looking as if he didn't really plan on doing anything.) Well I could pick up in our bedroom too so your mom wouldn't have to do that room either.

Devin:

Good dad, that will make her smile.

Like:

I do like your mother's smile.

Devin:

Me Too.

Like:

Don't spend too much time cleaning up. I still have a gig tonight.

Devin:

Dad maybe I could stay with Bece. He did say I could call him anytime.

Like:

We really don't know this kid Devin. I don't think it would be right to ask him could you stay with him tonight.

Devin:

He said he would be my big brother.

Like:

I know he did, but big brothers need heads up on what's going on too.

Devin:

Maybe you're right dad.

Like:
So go clean up then get cleaned up.

Devin:
Dad you're so funny. You said the same thing two times.

## *-SWITCH-*

*(We see the boys driving. Bece and Beep are riding together in his car and Woody is driving Cindy's car. Bece music is sounding really good. They are having fun, and everybody is moving with caution. Bece is leading and Woody is following. Bece and Beep starts to talk and Bece is not paying any attention to the fact that Woody is following him.)

Beep:
So how do you like it?

Bece:
It sounds pretty good.

Beep:
I told you we knew what we were doing… (Pause.) How does it feel to be the son of a star?

Bece:
(Pause.) It's nice I guess.

Beep:
What thats all it's nice?

Bece:
It wasn't always like this. We were a nice small family. Both my parents were workaholics.

Beep:
Where's your dad?

Bece:

I guess it was bound to happen one way or another. My dad was music and computer inclined and my mom was Miss Drama throughout her life that's what my grandmother calls her anyway.

Beep:

So how is your dad?

Bece:

I heard you the first time Beep. I just didn't want to answer you.

Beep:

Well don't. I didn't mean to conjure up any ill feelings.

Bece:

There are no ill feelings. My father is dead.

Beep:

Oh, I'm sorry man. I didn't know. I guess that's why everybody calls me Beep.

Bece:

Why because you always put your foot in your mouth? .. . It's okay man, it's okay.

Beep:

Thanks man call me Bartholomew, Bartholomew Lane.

Bece:

That's my dads' name. That's okay I'll call you Beep.

Beep:

(While looking back.) Cool, so where is Woody?

Bece:

(Looks back also.) I knew I was talking too much I forgot about Woody.

**\*-SWITCH 1977-\***

-\*(Eeshun is getting up off the bed.)-\*

Eeshun's Dad:
Where are you going Eeshun? You can't get away from me. I know everything about you, you even look just like me. So you can't run too far at all.

Eeshun:
Why are you doing this to me? I'm not afraid of you anymore. You use to have me all screwed in the head, like no one else wanted me but you. Well not any longer. I'll still rise.

Eeshun's Dad:
(Smacks her in the face.) You stubborn little bitch just like your mother. Couldn't nothing break her down easily either. But I'll get you. You are still young. Your mom was too old and like they say you can't teach an old dog new tricks.

Eeshun:
My momma was no dog and you will not treat me like one anymore. (She grabs a meat tenderizer out of her drawer and charges at him with all her heart and soul and beat the crap out of him, With the old meat tenderizer with the silver grooves. He gets up a little wobbly.)

Eeshun's Dad:
I'ma kill you bitch, I'ma kill you.

Eeshun:
(Grabs the keys off the table by the door, runs out of the house with all her might, jumps in the car and drives off full speed.)

*-Set everything up right. - *
**-Time switch 1999.-*

*(She never looked back. Eeshun was driving so fast and not thinking she ran a red light and almost caused an accident with Woody in Cindy's car.)*

Woody:
(Blows the horn.) Slow down lady (He holler this out the window.) before you kill the both of us.

# *-SWITCH- .*

*(At Like's house, he's sitting in a big comfy chair. He has fallen asleep.)* *-"TuFF" the high school play- 1979-*

Cindy:
You can do anything, if you put your heart into it.

Like:
People are always saying that, but it's not that easy.

Cindy:
I didn't say it was. Things can be "TuFF" to make you appreciate it a little more.

Like:
Well, what would you say if I told you that I want you and I always wanted you?

Cindy:
I'll say you're crazy.

Like:
Well, "TuFF" I guess I am crazy.

Cindy:
We can't be together.

Like:
Why not? (He wakes up slowly.-1999.) Cindy, Every time I have a crisis she's on my mind... Cindy.

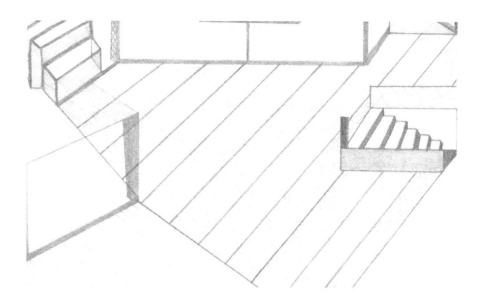

-*At Cindy's house*-

Cindy:
(Is looking in her closet at the same time and turns her head as if someone called her name.) That's strange.

## *-SWITCH-*

*(Time is ticking are we still tripping?)* *(Pete is still at airport. 1999.)*

Pete:
Okay ma'am I've been here four hours and still no friend.

Receptionist:
Well, maybe they took another route.

Pete:
Well, maybe they did.

Receptionist:
Would you like to use my phone to find out?

Pete:
Yes, I would (He dials the number.) Hey Tiggs how are you?

*-Over the phone-*

Tiggs:
Where are you I've called you all day.

*-Keep flip flopping-*

Pete:
Well, man I'm still here at the airport waiting on Day.

Receptionist:
(Eavesdropping.) Day is here sir.

Pete:
(Excited.) Where?

Receptionist:
(Understanding now that Day is a person not a time.) Sorry sir I thought you was talking about the time of DAY.

Pete:
No, I'm speaking about a man.

Receptionist:
Oh… my bad.

Pete:
(Back on phone.) Yeah, Tiggs does he have a cellphone, pager or any means of getting in touch with him?

Tiggs:
I really don't know Pete, but I do know we need to talk.

Pete:
What do we need to talk about?

Tiggs:
You and me.

Pete:
You and I? I thought we had everything under cover?

Receptionist:
(Gives a shocked face because she is listening to the conversation.)

Pete:
(Notice her reaction.) Listen, can we talk about this later on tonight?

Tiggs:
Not really Pete I have waited long enough.

Pete:
Well, wait a little longer and I'll see you tonight.

Tiggs:
I'm crazy about you Pete.

Pete:
(Pause. Looking over at lady.)

Tiggs:
Did you hear me Pete?

Pete:
(Trying to whisper.) I'm crazy about you too.

Tiggs:
Uh?

Pete
(Regular voice.) I'm crazy about you too! ... I must find Day Okay... (Hangs up.)

Receptionist:

(Not wanting him to say yes.) Do you need to use the phone again?

Pete:

No, no, no, thank you. (Walks away leaving the airport.)

### *-SWITCH-*

Bece:

We've been driving around for the last hour looking for Woody. Where could he be?

Beep:

Maybe he went on over to your house.

Bece:

Woody doesn't know where I stay.

Beep:

Who doesn't know where the superstar's house is?

Bece:

Why didn't you say anything earlier?

Beep:

The music was sounding really, really good man...

Bece:

Beep!?

Beep:

What!?

Bece:

Nothing, nothing.

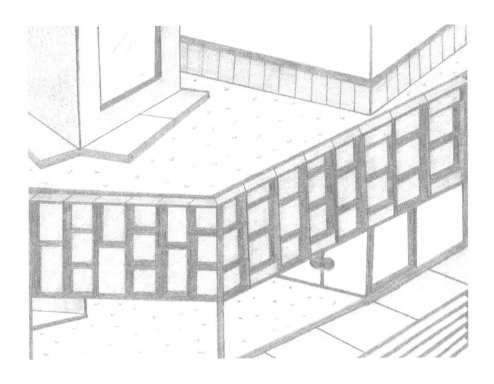

*-Fade Out-*

*(Back at Cindy's house. We hear Cindy in the shower trying to sing. Now we see Woody making his way up the stairs. He looks into different rooms until he spots Cindy's room. He enters with caution and is looking through her drawers. He spots a really nice red panty and bra set, and begins to sniff on them. We hear the shower water goes off and so does Woody. He runs out of her room with the set in his hands and hears the door about to open and ducks into Bece's room. Cindy opens the door and senses something is wrong, but didn't pay any attention to it. Cindy walks into her room and look into her drawer.)*

Cindy:
Now I just saw that red panty and bra set in this drawer. What's going on around here? (She walks out her room, down the stairs then Woody goes back into the room and throws the set under the bed with enough material showing so she would find it. We see Cindy looking into the kitchen drawer then grabs a butcher knife. She walks into the sunroom and Woody sneaks down the stairs and hides behind the grandfather clock. We see Cindy walking pass the clock and back up stairs. Woody takes to the kitchen through the sun room and out the window. Cindy is in her room and she looks out the window, she sees her car and makes her way down the stairs with the knife still in her hand, run through the living room, and opens the front door.) Bece is that you?

Woody:

No, Mrs. Chocolate it's me Woody. I was working on Bece's car today. We were following each other and I got left behind so I thought I should bring the car back.

Cindy:

(Not clear on his story.) Oh how nice of you to do that. Have you seen anyone out here?

Woody:

No ma'am just me... (Pause.) Did you have any plans with that kitchen knife?

Cindy:

I don't have any plans as long as you don't have any plans.

Woody:

No ma'am, I don't have any plans. I just wanted to know could I wait here for Bece, he'll be taking me home.

Cindy:

(Still looking around.). I guess so. Come in. Are you sure you didn't see anyone out here? (Cindy closes the door, but is looking at Woody as if she doesn't believe him.)

## *-SWITCH-*

*(We see Day outside of the train station. He looks a little tired and disheveled. He is sitting on his one big suitcase and he is holding his guitar. We see this car roll up on him at a light not on him exactly. Eeshun is in it. She is still crying a little and looking into the mirror trying to pull herself together, putting on make-up. Day head is down trying to catch his breath and a power nap until his next plan. The light changes, the car pulls off slowly, and Day head rises slowly too. Time is ticking and everybody knows there's not any to waste.)*

*(Like is at home looking at the piece of paper that Bece gave him and he is debating should he call him over to baby-sit? So he does.)*

Like:

(Dials Bece number.)

Cindy:
Hello.

Like:
Hi, is Bece in?

Cindy:
No, he's not in right now so please call him later. (She's not too relax while Woody is in the house.)

Like:
Okay thank you ma'am (Before he could finish she was gone. Then he hangs up.) Well dog she could have been a bit more pleasant.

*(Cut to Trish in office looking for Like's number and she finds it
and she starts for the phone. Cut back to Likes' house.)*

Like:
Are you almost finished son?

Devin:
Yes, sir. (He comes out of his room.) Dad I really like that kid.

Like:
He's not a kid, he's...

Devin
(Cuts him off.) I know that dad I just hear some of the older kids' saying it at my school.

Like:
Good at least you know.

Devin
Dad, what were you doing at Bece's age since that's your old high school?

Like:
I use to sing in the chorus or shall I say glee club, (We see pictures of him and his friends in chorus.) I use to be on the swim team, (We see all of them again.) and I performed a lot of plays and my favorite one was written by one of my classmates. (We see him and Cindy performing "TuFF".) I considered myself as a three-dimensional student with a lot to offer the world, but I stuck with the one thing that matters the most to me and that was anything musical related.

Devin:
Dad do you think you did enough? (Phone rings.)

Like:
Hello.

*-In office with Trish.-*

Trish:
Hi, Mr. Waters it's me Trish. I'm just calling to inform you that my big boss is coming to see you guys perform tonight. No pressure intended, but I do want you and your band to be extra good. Mr. Clearly doesn't get out to often to scout the upcoming groups. Do you have any questions?

*-At Like's house.-*

Like:
He's coming tonight?

Trish:
Yes.

Like:
Is he ready for a record deal?

Trish:
I wasn't going to mention that to you because I didn't want to add any pressure to the pressure that is already on.

Like:
What? So he is looking to sign a record deal?

Trish:
Let's not jump the gun Mr. Waters. We are looking for some new artists for an upcoming sound track for a motion picture.

Like:
Oh really now?

Trish:
Yes, so you might have to share the spotlight with some others, but yes we are looking to make some agreements/arrangements. You just do your best, and there's no telling what could happen tonight.

Like:
Thank you Ms. Spears. See you there.

Trish:
See ya. (Hangs up.)

*-(Cut to Like's house)-*

Like:
There is no telling what could happen tonight.

***-SWITCH-*** 

*(We find ourselves at Lady's house. She comes in with bags of groceries in her arms. She puts them down and goes to get something to drink with a smile on her face. She notices she has messages and she starts to listen to them, she smiles at her daughter's voice. She has a plan, since Lady is excited about her outcome at work. She'll tell her face to face.)

Lady:
(Out loud to herself.)
I know exactly where she's going tonight. I guess I'll go and have myself a drink too.

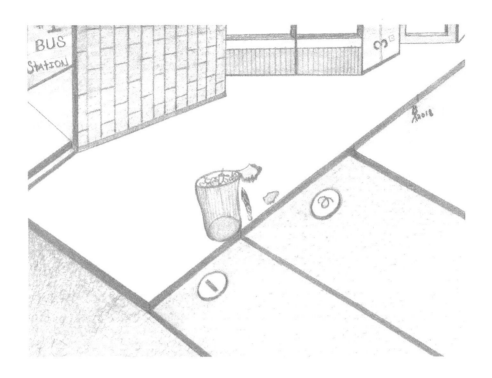

**\*-SWITCH-\***

*(Pete has left the airport. We see him driving around town looking for Day. In the car he has a big piece of paper that reads "Day Beens come with me". He stops at the Greyhound bus station, walks around holding the sign up for awhile. He has all types of people coming up to him saying they are Day Beens, but he doesn't believe anyone of them because he has a description of him in his head. That's if Like described him well. Then he starts to move on.)\*

**\*-SWITCH-\***

*(We are now at Eeshun's house. She is in the process of getting dressed. As she looks in the back of her closet for her shoes she stumbles upon an old cap and gown in a clear bag as if it's been sealed in time.-Switch- 1979.)\*

Day:
Well, don't you look nice?

Eeshun:
So do you.

Day:
Things are never going to be the same after tonight.

Eeshun:
I know.

Day:
Look, about what I said the other day, I didn't mean to be so ugly about it.

Eeshun:
It's okay this time. Maybe you are right I shouldn't be scared to live and grow.

Day:
Or be happy. We haven't told anyone around school that we are seeing each other.

Eeshun:
I just don't like everybody in my business.

Day:
We haven't even told Cindy. Now what's your excuse?

Eeshun:
I know Day. It's just some thing's you don't know about me, and I haven't shared them with Cindy either.

Day:
What are you holding back that you will just let me walk away and not even explain to me?

Eeshun:
Day, I can't tell you. I'm just going to have to stay here. Please understand…Go and enjoy life, accomplish all your goals and I'll be right here.

Day:
Why are you doing this to us'? (We hear the graduation march music begin.)

Teacher:
Okay graduating class of 1979, I've enjoyed each and every one of you. I wish everyone success. Things are not going to be easy in the real world, but it will be an experience you will never forget in your whole lifetime. Make good decisions and love with all your might because youth is not always on your side. (Crying a little.) Well, let me hush before I bore you too death on this special night.

Students:
We love you Mrs. Dean. (We see a shot of all the friends in line and giving each other the goo-goo eyes of unspoken words that just can't be said right now. We see Cindy looking at Eeshun, Day and Like. Like is checking out Cindy as if he wants to say something, but no one speaks.)

### *-SWITCH-*

Bece:
(Reaches home and see his mothers' car and he's not too happy about the whole situation. He enters with haste.) Mom! Woody! (He calls their names as he enters.)

Cindy:
I'm in here and I'm okay. Your friend Woody is in the kitchen eating on a sandwich and drinking on a soda.

Beep:
Hey again Mrs. Chocolate.

Cindy:
Hi. Please just call me Ms. C.

Beep:
Okay Ms. C. (Then the boys start to walk off.)

Cindy:
Bece, may I speak to you please? (As she says this we see Beep and Woody in the kitchen looking at Bece and Cindy. Bece's back is towards the kitchen and Cindy casually looks around him to look at the boys. She waves and smiles at the boys while she mutters.) The next time your friend comes inside my house uninvited I'ma kick his butt myself.

Bece:
(Startled.) Mom, who Woody?

Cindy:
Don't talk too loud, but yes him.

Bece:
Did he hurt you?

Cindy:
Nope, but I thought I was going to hurt him. Don't say anything, he seems like a good kid who might just got caught up in the moment.

Bece:
Yep, we are going to accept that excuse only once. I will always keep my eyes on the both of them.

Cindy:
I didn't mean to come between you and your friends.

Bece:
No friendship is lost. I'm still getting to know people and I'm not always clear about their motives. (They both turn to look at the boys and waved. Then Bece turn to his mom.) So you come first before any friends.

Cindy:
Thanks, baby. Well on that note Bece I'ma gone and leave and if Eeshun calls tell her I'll meet her there.

Bece:
Okay mom be careful out there it's a lot of crazy people in the world.

Cindy:
I will baby. (Gives him a kiss on his forehead.) And somebody called for you, but I didn't take a message.

Bece:

Okay. (Trying to help her out the house now because he knows she will keep on talking.) Bye.

Cindy:

(Is now standing on the porch. It is a beautiful night not too breezy, clear skies then she lifts her head to the sky and speaks.) I hope the Kennedy's are okay. Lord I ask you to please keep me and mine's under your divine protection. Amen.

**\*(It's about 8: o'clock now. The night has fallen a little darker, but not it's darkest, so be aware of the time.)\***

**\*-SWITCH-\***

\*(We see Pete pulling into the train station fast and deranged then he parks the car. Pete jumps out of car with sign in his hands, and the words on the sign are facing his body so Day can't read it. Day is looking at Pete as if he would like to ask him are you looking for me, but dared not to since he seems a little strange. Pete enters building and begins to hold up sign looking for Day. He walks around asking people are you Day Beens. Not getting anywhere this makes him more frustrated than anything. He storms out of the building all sad and pissed off looking as if he failed another mission given by the boys. And this makes him madder than hell. )

Pete:

(Screams.) Is there anybody named Day Beens out here? (People begin to look around.)

Day:
(Hesitates to answer, but he knows he should speak up before Pete explodes.) My name is Day Beens.

Pete:
Day Beens out of LA.? Who plays the guitar?

Day:
Yes that's me...

Pete:
Well good you can come with me please?

Day
Are you okay sir?

Pete:
Oh, I'm okay. I've only been looking for you all day, Day sir. Do you know what I mean? Do you have any bags or anything?

Day:
Yes.

Pete:
Do you need any help?

Day:
Oh, no, no, I've got it. Thanks.

Pete:
Well get in and lets go, we're late, you need a practice run and I need a break.

Day:
Sure, whatever you say man.
(Pete drives off.)

## *-SWITCH-*

(At Eeshun's house. We see her in a nice short silk robe with her face beat to a tee. She calls Cindy's house.)

Eeshun:
Hey, is that you Bece? Well good you got your moms' car back. What she's gone already. Oh she'll meet me there. Did she seem okay to you Bece? Good. She did what? She has on a trench coat, but why? You might be right, still hiding her outfits. I'm quite sure she's looking good. Well I need to finish getting dressed myself. Love you hon, I'll talk to you later.

## *-SWITCH-*

*(We are at Lady's house. We see her in a robe, make-up and her hair is done. She calls Cindy's house too.)*

Lady:
Hey Grandmama's baby. Get up horsy going to town to see Jaculyning knows bulk a bloc ka, bulk a bloc ka etc... Okay I won't sing that song to you anymore. I know you're too old to listen to lullabies.

(Pause.) Well, guess what they use to put you to sleep. Boy you are only sixteen. You are never too grown for your grandmother's lap, and you can ask your momma that. Where is your mom? Gone? Good. I guess she's gone to her old hang out the Ying Yang's? Well I just wanted you to know where I was going. Yep I'm going to the Yang's. I think it will be a nice surprise too baby. If you need me I'll be there okay. Love you baby boy Bye.

## *-SWITCH-*

*(We see Tiggs is already at the club. There is a nice crowd out tonight. We see the roadies setting up the stage. The DJ is spending the records and people are dancing and having fun. Tiggs is nervous because he doesn't know what to expect tonight then Like walks in with Devin.)

Tiggs:
What's up with you Like?

Like:
(Pulls him close.) Melody left today. She said she needs to catch her breath, so hey what can I say?

Tiggs:
What are we going to do with Devin?

Like:
Let him hang out like he does in rehearsals.

Tiggs:
Well this ain't rehearsal and it's a lot more that goes on during club time.

Like:
I know Tiggs. You just let me handle this. Where's Pete, Hell where's Day?

Tiggs:
They haven't got here yet, but I'm quite sure they're on the way.

Like:
They better be. It's already been enough stress for one day..

Tiggs:
(Turns to walk and look out of the front door.) You are right about that.

Like:
(Stopping Tiggs dead in his tracks.) Hey Tiggs don't go too far, I need your help to watch Devin.

Tiggs:
I knew it, I knew it, I knew it…

**\*-SWITCH-\***

*(We see Cindy in the car riding through the city. We see her reach for the sun visor to bring it down and second guess her actions. She thumbs through some cassettes

then she reaches in her glove compartment and takes out one tape. She looks at it long and hard then slips it into the cassette player, and she begins to hold the stirring wheel tighter with both hands. We hear the messages from the tape begins.)*

Lady:
It's me Hon just letting you know I made it home. Love y'all.

Eeshun:
Call me girl I got some good news, and kiss my nephew for me, hi BC.

Bartholomew Carson Jones:
Bece and Cindy it's me. I love you baby. I love both my babies. Enjoy life and keep things right and I will always be in the light…
(Cindy snatches the tape out with all her might.)

Cindy:
Well honey we made it. It's your anniversary and I've tried not to dwell on it too long today. I had this dream that I couldn't put together at first and now I can. I saw you John, Carolyn, and Lauren all on one plane together I really don't know if they are about to join you or what. So look out for each other. Listen to me. I still talk to you as if you are here. I love you BC Jones and yes I know that life goes on. See ya.

## *-SWITCH-*

*(Day and Pete arrives at the club.).*

Pete:
I'm sorry Mr. Day about my earlier behavior.

Day:
It's okay I'm quite sure we both have had a stressful day.

Pete:
Just a lot of unsolved mysteries in the ATL. (They both laughs.)

Day:
I agree with that. (He's getting out of the car now.) Are you coming?

Pete:
I'll be in there soon, okay.

Day:
Okay. Thanks for the ride lady. (Like the movie creep show.)

Pete:
(Gives him this look of you better be kidding.)

Day:
Don't take it so serious man. Just kidding, but thanks for the ride, really.

Pete:
No problem.

*(Pete sits there a little while longer. -SWITCH-)*

*Day is inside the club.*

Tiggs:
Mr. Beens you made it, good to see you. Mr. Waters is going to be so happy. I'll go get him. Where is Mr. Rosalyn?

Day:
Who?

Tiggs:
Pete?

Day:
Oh he's out in the car. Is he okay?

Tiggs:
I'll go and see in a minute, but I'm going to get Like right now...

Day:
Excuse me sir I really didn't catch your name.

Tiggs:
Tiggs just call me Tiggs.

Day:
Thank you Mr. Tiggs, tell Mr. Waters that I don't have all day to wait for him.

*(We see Cindy makes her way into the parking lot, drives around looking for Eeshun. Then goes to their regular parking spot. Pete is still in his car rumbling around, he is not causing a scene, but he is on a mission. Cindy spots him in his car and she puts on her extra cautious senses. Just being aware of her surroundings.)*

*-Back inside of the club.-*

Devin:
Dad, can I sit on the stage with you?

Like:
No, son you may not. (Walks up to Day.) Hey Day oh my goodness it is so good to see you. How has life been treating you?

Day:
(Shakes Devin's hand and Hugs Like)

Good man. I can't say it's been the most enjoyable ride ever, but it's been good. How's life been treating you?

Like:
So far no complaints, but we do need to get you a little ready for tonight.

Day:
People are already here. I don't think practice will be necessary. I'll just go by the music. I still know how to read sheet music.

Like:
Are you sure? I know that you enjoy playing by feelings.

Day:
I'm sure. When in the Atl, you do what the Atlaliens do.

Like:
Stick around for awhile this time. We have a lot of catching up to do. And if you do have to leave say good bye at least.

Day:
Sure thing.

Devin:
Dad what's that blue stuff that lady is drinking?

Like:
Come on Devin, I might call Bece back anyway. (About to walk off with Devin.)

Devin:
(Looks back at Day.) Good. (With a conquering smile and wave.)

Day:
(He waves his pointing finger as to tell with a smile.)

### *-SWITCH-*

*(At Bece's house. We see Bece and Woody playing video games and Beep is looking at a Playboy/Penthouse magazine. The telephone rings.)*

Bece:
Hello. (Split Screen.)

Like:
Hello is Bece in?

Bece:
Yes this is he.

Like:
Hi Bece this is Mr. Waters, we met earlier today at the high school.

Bece:
Hi Mr. Waters I know who you are. What's up?

Like:
I was calling to see were you busy tonight?

Bece:
(He looks around.) Nope, not too busy.

Like:
I know this is such a short notice or shall I say no notice at all, but I wanted to know if you could keep Devin for a couple of hours, until I finish my gig tonight?

Bece:
I didn't know you were in the business Mr. Waters. Sure I could keep him. Where are you guys?

Like:
We're at this old whole in a wall club, but it's really nice...

Bece:
(Before he could finish Bece speaks out.) Ying Yang's.

Like:
Whatcha you know about the Ying Yang's?

Bece:
That's my moms' old hang out. She's suppose to be there tonight, I guess to watch you perform.

Like:
I guess I'll have to meet the lady who raised such a fine chap.

Bece:
Okay Mr. Waters you're letting your true age shine through now. I'll be there soon.

Like:
Thanks, and how much do I owe you?

Bece:
I'll let you decide that, you've been sixteen before.

Like:
Okay then.

Bece:
Okay, bye.

Like:
Bye. (Looks at Devin.) Get your things together Bece is coming to get you. And please don't' take him the scenic route home.

Devin:
But why Dad?

Like:
It's too late.

### *-SWITCH-*

*(Back in the parking lot we see Eeshun pulls in. She drives around for a second, but she makes her way to their regular parking spaces too. She parks, and Cindy jumps out of her car into Eeshun's car.

Eeshun:
Are you okay?

Cindy:
Girl, I'm fine I was just ready to leave the house.

Eeshun:
Are you ready to chill and have fun like the old days?

Cindy:
I thought you would never ask.

Eeshun:
(Pulls out a cigarette looking thing and begins to fire it up.) And hey don't talk too much.

Cindy:
You know me I've been working on my hold and release.

Eeshun:
Good. Shhh. (There's a knock at the window.)

Voice:
Freeze Police. (The girls almost jump out of their skin.)

Lady:
Y'all still doing the same old stuff. I told you that was going to get y'all in trouble. Now get out or there before the police come for real.

Cindy:
Mom what are you doing here?

Lady:
I had such a wonderful day that I wanted to come and hang out, have a toast, and listen to some good music with my favorite girls. (They get out the car slowly and slightly disappointed.)

Eeshun:
(Gives her a hug and a kiss.) Good to see you Momma C.

Lady:

Hey don't act like we're strangers this long anymore. You can come by and see me you don't need Cindy with you.

Eeshun:

Yes, ma'am. (They are all walking down the alley to the club door.)

Cindy:

(Looks at her mom.) I assume the banquet was a hit?

Lady:

Yep, but we're not here to talk about that so I'll tell you later.

Eeshun:

The first round or drinks are on me.

Cindy:

The last one's on me.

Lady:

So I'll take the in between round. (As they approach the door a car drives past them and we see Mr. Clearly on the passenger side and Trish is driving. Mr. Clearly and Lady catches each others eye.) ...

Cindy:

(She notices this.) Come on momma you are hanging out a little too much already.

Lady:

I'm never too old to flirt.

Cindy:

Something must have happen today because you wouldn't have said that last week.

Lady:

(Smiles and walk in.) As they enter without any charges, we see various of people and things going on. People are dancing and mingling. We see a visiting band playing before the headliners. The bartender who was here earlier notices Cindy Chocolate in the house. So he makes his way over quite quickly.

Bartender:
Mrs. Chocolate, ladies good evening.

Ladies:
Hi, good evening.

Bartender:
If you need anything just call on me. (They arrive to the table now.)

Eeshun:
Could we get three White Zin fandels please?

Bartender:
Sure and enjoy your evening.

The ladies:
(All begin to take off their small lite weight coverings, jackets, shawls etc...and notice that they all have on red. They all laugh.)

Cindy:
It never fails…

Cindy & Eeshun:
We always feel each other.

Lady:
I guess I must be in sync tonight too.

*(We now see Clearly and Spears walk in together.)*

Lady:
(The only one turned facing the door. Girls backs are to the door.) mmmm, they get younger and younger.

Girls:
What you say mom?

Lady:
Nothing.

> *(Lady, sees Clearly/Spears stop to talk with Like and Day, but the girls don't see a thang and momma don't know them too well to even care. We now see Trish leading the way to the back, and Clearly slowly walking, looking for someone, spots Lady sitting at the table with her friends. They are talking and sipping on wine. We notice that Cindy sees him pass and follow him to his spot with her eyes, she sees a little boy sitting at a table coloring and thought out loud to herself.

Cindy:
Umph how odd.

The Ladies:
What you say?

Cindy:
Nothing, nothing.

> *(Now we hear the guest band ending their set, playing their last song and giving their thanks. We see a small huddle starting to form up front by the stage.

Like:
Tiggs, where's Pete?

Day:
The guy who picked me up?

Like:
Yep where is he?

Day:
He's in the band?

Tiggs:

Yes he is. Like what's it to you. (On the defense.)

Day:

Get off my back. He just seemed a little stressed to me that's all.

Tiggs:

He must be still out in the parking lot. Like, I'll go get him. (As soon as Tiggs got the words out his mouth, in walks Pete. Tiggs is shocked and surprised.) Pete!?

Day & Like:

(Turned around, eyes bucked wide open, like she was one of the most beautiful women they've ever seen... In a long time.)

Day & Like:

Pete!?

Pete:

(Has on red.) Look, Mr. Waters I've been lying to you a little too long, but I've help get us this far so please just listen to me. I couldn't get a steady gig playing in a band and I couldn't figure out why... I played the drums like a pro better than any guy I know and I couldn't find a job nowhere. So Tiggs my boyfriend said you really needed a drummer, but he said that you didn'tt want a female because you didn't want to mess up the flow. I couldn't lose any job without trying so I became Pete Rosalyn, but my real Name is Rosalyn Renee Sharron Pete. Of Pete's Upholstery King, so please don't fire me Mr. Waters.

Like:

(Shocked & surprised.)

You are an excellent drummer Pete, I mean Rosalyn and I'll be a fool to let you go. It's just that they came to see an all guy band...

Tiggs:

It will be okay Mr. Waters. I'm sure by the time they even second-guess us they'll see how well she plays.

Pete:
He is so supportive Mr. Waters. We won't let you down.

Like:
Sure. No other choice. She is good. The gig must go on.

*(By this time we see Bece making his way through the crowd walking right pass Mr. Waters and crew. Bece also walks pass his mom and her girls trying to get to Devin. They are eating now so they didn't see him either. We see Bece at Devin's table and now he's looking around for his momma and them. Now Cindy spots Bece.)*

Cindy:
Hold on y'all, I see Bece.

The Ladies:
What, where?

Cindy:
I'll be back. (Walks over to the boys.) What are you doing here?

Bece:
I'm giving back.

Cindy:
What are you talking about?

Bece:
Mom I would like for you to meet Mr. Devin Waters.

Cindy:
(Turns to look at him in awe.) Who?

Bece:
Mr. Devin Waters. (Devin holds out his hand.)

Devin:
Nice to meet you Mrs. Bece momma…

Cindy:
(Shakes his hand.)

Bece:
(Continues to talk.) I met them at school and his daddy needed a baby sitter tonight so I'm here.

Cindy:
His daddy?

***(Walking up from behind Cindy, speaking.)***

Like:
I'm his daddy. Nice to meet you Mrs. Jones. (Hand extended out.)

***(Cindy turns around and their eyes locked. By now, Eeshun is all up in their mix, not on purpose, it's taking Cindy a little too long to get back over to them. So she's standing on the footrest connected to the barstool with her bad ankle. She begins to slip a little off the chair and before she could fall and loose any cool points there was a helping hand to break her fall. While she was slipping a little she was looking down and all see could see are a pair of shoes. *(Flashback to school's play scene at the bottom of the stairs, where she sees a pair of shoes.)* before she could look up to gather her composure)*.**

Eeshun:
Thank you, thank you. (Now, looks him dead in his eyes.) Day!?

Day:
Miss Wells!?

Like:
Cindy!?

Cindy:
Like!?

Lady:
(Walks over and looks at Like and Cindy.) Well, well the group is back together.

Bece:
Hey grandma! (We see Mr. Clearly and Trish looking on.) …

Cindy:
(Turns and looks at Bece and Devin.) Well, Bece if you're keeping Devin I think you should be leaving.

Bece:
Mom, do you know Mr. Waters?

Like:
You could say that.

Bece:
Well let's go Devin things are getting a little hectic around here.

Devin:
I'm riding with you big brother.

Like & Cindy:
Y'all be careful. (Together they turn and looked at each other.)

Cindy:
Ain't nothing changed.

Like:
Not one bit.

Trish:
(Comes down to speak to Like) Are you all ready?

Day:
(Looks at Eeshun.) Don't you move I've waited a long time to see you face to face again!

Eeshun:
The next place I'm going is with you!

Day:
I'll hold you to it! (They begin to walk towards the stage. Like looks at Cindy, they speak to each other with their eyes and Cindy knows she'll be right there once Like finishes.)

Trish:
Excuse me ladies my boss would love to treat you all to a bottle of the finest wine in the house.

Lady:
Does your boss have a name?

Trish:
Mr. David Clearly is his name ma'am and yourself?

Lady:
Lady, Lady Charlatan.

Cindy & Eeshun:
Call her Lady.

Trish:
Thanks Mrs. C. (She turns to Cindy) I finally get an opportunity to meet you in person Mrs. Cindy Chocolate. I'm Trish Spears and I'm actually indirectly working for you too.

Eeshun:
Looking for new music are we?

Trish:
You guessed it right!

Cindy:
Oh you are working on the movie sound track.

Trish:
Yes ma 'am (Now turns to look at Lady) and I think my boss is flirting with you. (Lady's not paying any attention to Trish. She's looking at David now.)

Eeshun:
Mom, I think she's talking to you.

Cindy:
I believe she already knows this. Tell your boss we'll take another bottle of White Zinfandel… He can come over to ask my mom for a dance sooner or later. Thank you!

**\*(We hear the music being performed and it's an awesome concert. Pete showed off especially on her solo the crowd went wild to see that lady on fire. Day and Like played songs and rapped with so much passion that Cindy and Eeshun just knew that they were singing, rapping, and playing to them.**

**They were laughing, blushing and thinking nasty sexy thoughts about the boys. They knew this time that they wasn't going to let them get away. Now we see Lady and Mr. Clearly on the dance floor cutting the rug. Everybody**

**was a little tipsy, but not drunk they were having good clean fun that was well over due for. Good and everything was good. The party is now over.)\***

Like:
I would like to thank everybody for coming out and giving up so much love and support. That's the only way to be. (Announces band members.) Be safe and see you next week.

Cindy:
Something told me to drive.

Eeshun:
Yep, yep, yep and I'm glad you drove too. Day will be coming with me.

Cindy:
Oh my goodness listen to us talking about them like they are a piece of meat.

Eeshun:
You best believe they are thinking about us the same way. (They both look at the guys and the guys are in deep conversation, but the guys look their way as if they heard them. Then the girls laugh.)

Cindy:
It looks as if Like is wearing a wedding ring.

Eeshun:
Look C. you still wear yours.

Cindy:
You are right, but I don't think his wife is dead.

Eeshun:
Let's not jump to any conclusions that will only mess up the moment. Talk to him that's all you have to do. Just tell him all the things you didn't get to tell him in high school.

### *-SWITCH GUY TALK-*

Like:
Good she's married, how I feel right now that's the only thing that will save us. Or stop me one or the other.

Day:
They haven't even changed a bit.

Like:
Oh you're not angry with her anymore?

Day:
Too much time has passed to even remember what I was mad about.

Like:
Let's do the right thing we are all grown ups now so we must think about the repercussions of our actions.

Day:
Okay daddy, Devin left about three hours ago.

Like:
My bad man. (David and Trish walk over.)

David Clearly:
That was very impressive if I shall say so myself.

Both:
Thank you!

David Clearly:
Have you all work together long?

Like:
No, but we are familiar with each other's music and style.

Day:
We went to high school together.

Like:
You look familiar Mr. Clearly.

David Clearly:
Good because you will be hearing and seeing a lot more of me soon. We can talk business later. Trish, she knows how to get in touch with you?

Like:
Yes, sir.

Clearly:
(Addressing Day.) And you sir?

Day:
Just call me Day.

Clearly:
A lot of peaceful things happen in the day Mr. Day so, don't go too far yourself.

Day:
Sure. (Lady comes over to speak.)

Lady:
It's so good to see you two again. You all have barely changed. Listen. (Coming in a little closer to the guys.) Those are some sweet ladies not girls, but ladies over there so be careful of your...

All:
Actions!

Lady:
Yep y'all still smart too.

Guys:
(They both give her a big hug with all their might.)

Lady:

I can't breathe. (They let her go.) Take care of each other boys. Are you ready Mr.Clearly? I'll be dropping you off and that's all.

***(Now we only see the four friends standing.)***

Cindy:

It really feels like old times again. (As the camera pans around the four of them they are all young again at their last senior dance with their outfits on that so happens to look like their style in their older age. Colors are the same too, to keep things in sync.)

Eeshun:

(Breaks up that thought, very quickly. They are back in the present now.) Excuse me everybody but since we are friends will it be okay if I talk with my friend alone?

Day:

Are you talking about Cindy or me?

Eeshun:

You fool. I see Cindy all the time.

Cindy:

Funny how men can come between friends.

Day:

Like, do you need my help?

Like:

No, I got it. You go and enjoy yourself. It was nice seeing you again Eeshun and next time don't let the break period be so long.

Eeshun:

(Walking to him with open arms.) You are absolutely correct. It is good seeing you again and believe me we now know how to find you. (She gives him a big hug.)

Cindy:
(Acts as if she's clearing her throat.)
Get your hand off my man.

Like & Eeshun:
Okay bye, bye.

Day:
I guess I better get me a hug in too CC or shall I say Mrs. Cindy Chocolate? (They hug.) I liked your last movie. I always say to myself I remember when that's all she ever talked about was acting and you did it.

Cindy:
It seems like we all stuck to our goals. So we all can say we did it!

Everybody:
We did it! (Day and Eeshun leaves.)

Like:
(Is packing up some of the thing that were left out, trying not to get too close to Cindy.)

Cindy:
Eeshun said I should come right out and tell you what I should have told you twenty years ago.

Like:
May be we shouldn't mention too much since we're both married.

Cindy:
Yes and no. My husband is (Pause) dead.

Like:
Come, come I'm sorry Cindy. I just want to hold you so close that my heart aches. I've been thinking about you since the night we graduated. You drive me crazy then I see you on film then I drive by your summer home then I look in the yearbook... (Before he could finish speaking she steps in verbally.)

Cindy:

(Begins with.) I thought we weren't going to say too much. (But since we are I have something to say too type of feeling going on. Pacing.) Listen, Like everything we have ever shared together in our short years in high school has made me an awesome person inside and out. (She is so excited and tongue tide about what she's trying to say that it makes her angry. She continues.) I don't know what I'm trying to say. All I know is I'm crazy about you and I can't shake these feelings. I thought that after we graduated it was going to go away like good old fashion puppy love. But it didn't, I went to college met a wonderful man, married him, had a son, enjoyed a short-lived life with him and now I'm raising Bece. We loved him dearly and we still do, but you have always been present. It doesn't mean I didn't love my husband. I guess you're the bike I didn't get a chance to ride.

Like:

(Tries to hold her again. It's a little too much for her to handle right now, but he doesn't give up the pursuit. He keeps it calm and easy then she finds herself sinking into his arms. He kisses her forehead, she exhales, he kisses her face, cheeks, ears, nose, and then her lips. *Note they have never kissed before.• So it is shocking to feel the power or both their lips together, but it doesn't stop them at all. They squeeze each other a little closer then out of nowhere Like lifts Cindy onto the stage.)

Like:
Turn around so I can get a better look at you.

Cindy:
(As she turn slowly.) Where's your wife?

Like:
Well this may sound like a tired typical man response. (Trying to explain.)

Cindy:
Some lady must have called you that before?

Like:
Only about once or twice in my life time, but seriously she left this morning to take a break from the real world, that's me and Devin, to catch her breath and that's okay. I know that everybody needs a break once in awhile. So I guess she'll return to us soon.

Cindy:
Well, should I leave?

Like:
Nope, we are both on a break. And believe me, you are one of the nicest breaks I've ever had.

Cindy:
I'm glad you didn't use some old tired typical man reply.

Like:
I was trying to avoid one.

Both:
(Speak but didn't know this was the way both of them felt.) I love you Cindy. (Heard first.) I love you Like. (Heard second.) (But together.)

Cindy:

Don't flatter yourself Like I was very much in love with Bece's father, but it was like I really didn't get a chance to express my feelings to you. I was too much...

Like:

(Cuts in.)
You weren't too much of anything Miss Drama. You just always kept your eyes on the prize.

Cindy:

(Looks around the place.) And like you didn't?

Like:

Well, I let one prize get away by being young and dumb. So I knew from then on out that I was going to stay focus, and I did.

Cindy:

(Moves in closer on him like a sexy Black Panther.)
So am I the first prize you let slip away? (Clutching him in her paws, but gently like.)

Like:

(Sexy and charming as always.)
Of course you are... But if it's safe to say?

Cindy:

(Can't wait for him to say.) It's safe to say.

Like:

Not tonight. I want you.

**They begin to kiss and embrace each other so passionately that we can feel their serenity for each other. Genuine feelings shine through these two.**

**\*-SWITCH-\***

*(At Eeshun's house.)*

Eeshun
Today must have been meant to be.

Day:
I guess I can say that now.

Eeshun:
Why you say that?

Day:
Either Everything Was Wrong From the Git -Go or Right From the Start. It started off like a bad dream and I've awakened to be in your presence. That's an excellent ending to me.

Eeshun:
Day it's something I need to tell you to put closure to our high school days and why I couldn't go with you.

Day:
Baby don't worry about that.

Eeshun:
I want to. I need to get it off my chest. I felt like I didn't give you what you deserved at the time. Day my mother died when I was fourteen and my dad kinda started treating me as if I was my mother.

Day:
(Being goofy.)
He gave you too many chores?

Eeshun:
Don't be funny right now Day. (He notices how serious she is.) He started asking for kisses, rubdowns, bring him things while he was in the tub, and feed him breakfast in the bed in the mornings. I wanted to run, I wanted to date you openly, I wanted to hide my face, I wanted to be someone else period, anybody other than Eeshun Wells. I wasn't and I couldn't, so I didn't.

Day:
Oh my God "EE" I didn't know you was going through all of this.

Eeshun:
Nobody knew not even Cindy.

Day:
Miss Wells I'm here to tell you that nothing like that will go on in these parks again. (In his heaviest country boy voice ever. He grabs and holds on to her to seal the agreement.)

Eeshun:
So you don't think any less of me?

Day:
No. When we actually started talking, hanging out and sneaking around, it seemed like you were really being yourself. You made me laugh, you always kept me on my toes and you knew all the hottest spots in Georgia. I enjoyed watching you bloom from the ninth grade to the 12th grade, now look at you surviving and striving and most definitely styling in your thirties. How could I dare come back here and walk on your turf and tell you that I think any less of you. You are my QUEEN and I never even gotten married because I

haven't found anyone to compare or contrast you to, and I can honestly say that it hasn't been that great without you. So here on this descending evening of July 17th 1999 I, Day Early Beens ask Eeshun don't know your middle name Wells will you marry me?

The song house version of "All I Do Is Think About You" is playing on radio.

(He is on bended knee. He's doing it the right way.)

Eeshun:
(Mouth drops wide open with great surprise.)
Yes, Yes, Yes…and it's Denise, Early. (They smile, kiss and embrace each other.)

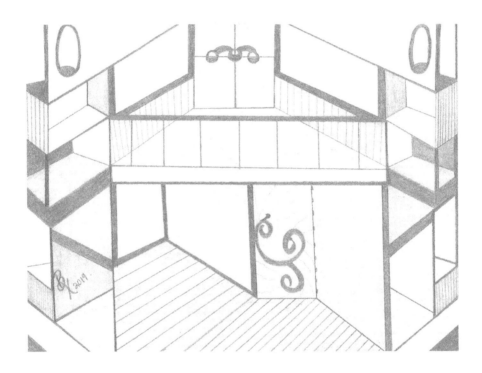

**\*-SWITCH-\***

Lady:
Well, here we are in one piece Mr. Clearly.

Clearly:
Would you like to come in for a night cap?

Lady:
Now Mr. Clearly you know I'm a lady and it's too late for me to be in your house.

Clearly:
Well I could show you my in home studio.

Lady:
Well technically that isn't your house then.

Clearly:
(He knows he's won here over.) Good.

Lady:
Don't get too happy Mr. Clearly. I'm only having one drink and my daughter knows where I am.

Clearly:
I just want to be in your presence. Good that she knows.

### *-SWITCH-*

Devin:
How does your mom know my dad?

Bece:
That's the same thing I'm wondering. (Under his breath so Devin couldn't hear.) And how well? (Continue in normal voice.) Auntie "EE" knew the other guy too.

Devin:
Maybe they work together.

Bece:
Nope, I've never seen your dad on a set.

Devin:
Maybe they went to school together.

Bece:

(Snaps his finger.) You are right. Do you all have a house library? My mom went to the same school.

Devin:

Sure follow me. (They entered a room full of books.) Right here.

Bece:

(Stands there and looks around.) Devin I'm really not trying to be nosy I just want to know did they all go there at the same time. There's the yearbook of 1979. (He and Devin sits there together and begin to thumb through the pages one by one. They both laugh a couple of times.) Do you like sports Devin?

Devin:

Yes I do my favorite is soccer.

**(The camera slowly pulls away from the two boys as to leave the room still focused on them as they bond.)**

**\*(-SWITCH-)\***

(Like and Cindy are in a full passionate bloom. Cindy is on one of the tall table stools and Like is between her legs, he is stroking back and fourth with clothes on. Then we see Cindy pull away gently and walk over to the stage.)

Cindy:

I want to be where you were singing to me. (He strolls over there, jumps on the stage with her and they begin to sing "All I Do Is Think About You", and they are dancing together. They sing as much as they know then the sadness begins to fill the room.)

Like:

Cindy what's wrong?

**\*(Changing the subject.)\***

Cindy:

(Takes a seat on the stage edge.) Why did your mom name you Like?

Like:
(He sits down beside her.) You're the first person after all these years to ever ask me that. Why you ask?

Cindy:
People usually name their kids after who, what, when and how they are feeling and sometimes why they are feeling it.

Like:
Well, there is a story behind it, but it's a long one so I hope you got the time since you asked?

Cindy:
I'm listening.

Like:
Well my mom and dad had been married for awhile and they had come to a troubled point in their lives around the fifth year. So they separated for awhile and my mother was dating a colored man as they called us back in the day so no one knew about the relationship. It didn't last long because she knew that she didn't really want to leave her husband, my dad, but she was starting to contemplate it because she was falling in love with this new guy. They broke up, she returned back to her husband and continued like nothing happened until 9 months later. I was born and my daddy was so happy to find out that they were having a little boy , he could hardly see straight. But he did notice that I wasn't the same race as he and my mother was totally relieved and surprise. Dad wasn't too upset because he knew he did his share in the separation too and he couldn't fault her for her outcome of it. But he didn't think that he could LOVE the little baby boy with all his heart so they named me Like Waters.

Cindy:
I'm speechless, I didn't know.

Like:
Oh, it's okay. It was a period of adjustment, but we made it through... So tell me something about you?

Cindy:
What?

Like:
How did you meet Bece's father when you were suppose to be so crazy about me?

Cindy:
I was crazy about you. But since we never really said anything about it I just kept on living. So I met him while I was in college. Bartholomew Carson Jones was a very, very nice man and he didn't think like a college man. Everything he wanted to complete he worked hard at it. I could hardly keep up with him, he was always on a mission, and I guess in a sense that kept me in tune with him because he released so much positive energy that it took my breath away. So we were married sophomore year of college. You couldn't pull us apart. Bart studied Double Ett some computer nerd stuff, but he was not goofy he made being smart cool. I of course majored, studied, practice, lived, ate and slept drama from stage to film. I knew the behind scenes, but I lone to be in front of the camera. We finished college and enjoyed a year of vacation time of just the two of us and then a bundle of joy was knocking at our door. We named him Bece Bryce Jones because Bartholomew Carson Jones was too long and we thought it would be too much pressure for a son to try to live up to his father's name. Bart went on to be an excellent computer man, open his own business and added a drama studio in the building so Bece and I could be close to him. We were heading in the right direction for a long time I guess about four-years or so. Bart had join together many different things and made them work. Movie sound tracks, rappers, RB singers, and training school for the computer heads. This had all come together in this one place of business. Bart was burning the candle at both ends he was flying in and out of the city. Then one lovely long hot day of summer of 1989 July 16th Bart was making a journey back home leaving New York City assuring a role for his wife , me of course , to be in an upcoming stage production I had performed in during high school, you remember. I was Ruth in "A Raisin in the Sun" , it was one of my favorite roles ever and he knew it. The play was to run for 8 weeks at the Boardwalk Playhouse in Manhattan. I thought it was a business trip for the company and not for me. He never made it back home his plane went down in route. Bart being the type of man he was took his last moments of life to call Bece and I to tell us that he loves us. (We cut to the scene in the car and Cindy is listening to the tape.) Bece and Cindy it's me. I love you baby. I love both my babies. Enjoy life and keep things right and I will always be in the light. (Back in club with Like.) And I still have the tape. So I guess I be in this slump every year because I feel like I had something to do with his death and I keep on working because he truly believed in my dreams.

Thank you baby.

Like:
Oh Cindy you are a good person and you deserve goodness. It's really not hard to fall in love with you either.

Cindy:
Yep, the hard part is trying not to fall in love anymore and go on with life.

Like:
We need love.

Cindy:
You are absolutely right. But what about us who lose their loves and it's hard to continue on because we feel like no one is going to ever love us like that again?

Like:
Keep living and enjoy life, and if it's not anyone else this lifetime it will be in another one.

Cindy:
You always said that our souls have been here before and they shall pass through again.

Like:
And they did.

Cindy:
(Really looking at him.) And they did.
Both (Before they kiss.) You drive me crazy.

## *-SWITCH-*

**We see Eeshun and Day in the bed. Their upper body is nude covered in the right places.**

Eeshun:
Day I want to keep my last name.

Day:
Okay, But you do know that your last name will be Wells-Beens..

Eeshun:
That's just in case anybody asks. I'll just let them know I'm in good hands.

Day:
Okay, then I'll be Day Beens-Wells, just in case anybody asks me.

Eeshun:
Okay, now I'll hold you to it.

### *-SWITCH-*

***(We see Lady knocked out sleep on a big comfy chair. David Clearly brings over some cover and places it on Lady. Then he proceeds to lie beside her to fall asleep. We see an empty bottle of champagne on the table, we hear some soft music playing and they look so peaceful. We hear the music stop playing and slowly Lady's eyes starts to open. She notice that she's still at Mr. Clearly house, and she has some cover over her she accepts and acknowledge the fact that she might as well stay on over, and pulls the cover up over her ears. Then falls back to sleep. Then David wakes up glad to see she stayed and places his hand gently on her hip and falls back to sleep.**

### *-SWITCH-*

*(We pan all through Like's house like we are looking for something slowly. We are now in Devin's room with him and Bece.)*

Devin:
Can I go to sleep now?

Bece:
Oh sure I didn't know I was keeping you awake.

Devin:
I'm not use to all this excitement in one day.

Bece:
Me either.

Devin:
And I'm not use to having a big brother either.

Bece:
Well, I hope I don't let you down 'cause I don't have any siblings myself.

Devin:
We can learn together.

Bece:
But it will be at a slightly different pace.

Devin:
I know you can't teach me about girls yet.

Bece:
Believe me it will take more than just a day to figure them out.

**\*-SWITCH-\***

*(We see Tiggs and Rosalyn in bed.)*

Tiggs:
You did it baby.

Rosalyn:
I know. But I couldn't have pulled it off without you.

Tiggs:
You played better than Pete tonight.

Rosalyn:
I thought that since I was killing him off he should have a hella of a good-bye party tonight.

Tiggs:
Well you impressed me big time and I couldn't figure out how to tell you that I wanted him out our lives for good.

Rosalyn:
Why?

Tiggs:
I couldn't figure out was I loving Rosalyn or Pete.

Rosalyn:
(Reaches under the bed brings out the mustache and hat.) Let's see how well you can love both Pete and Rosalyn at the same time.

Tiggs:
(Begins to kiss her with the mustache on then he thinks twice.) Without the mustache but you can keep the hat on…

Rosalyn:
If it can stay on.

**\*-SWITCH-\***

**\*(We see Cindy and Like again, this time they are asleep with their clothes on and they are on this comfy couch. Cindy wakes up first, she looks around and they are lovely entwined into each other like they were really, really meant to be. So she holds on a little tighter because she knows that soon, all of this will have to end.**

Like:
I know you are awake already.

Cindy:
I know it can't last forever!

Like:
We could try.

Cindy:

Yeah, and if that was the case , Bece would be living with Devin and your wife. (They both half giggle.)

Like:

I guess we better snap back into reality then.

Cindy:

Yeah, (Looks out window.) Day has already broken, and we both would have to do a little too much explaining if it get any later. (Getting ready to leave.)

Like:

Wait Cindy is this our last time seeing each other?

Cindy:

Not if the Lord can help it.

Like:

We can still give him a hand though.

Cindy:

I'm quite sure we will.

Like:

You know our eyes locked...

Cindy:

And someone throw away the key.

**(Cindy bends down and pretends to pick up a key.)**
I'll hold on to it, until we meet again.
**(They stare at each other so hard they both begin to melt.
They hold each other until silence falls upon them.)**

Cindy:

I better leave.

Like:

I'll walk you.

***They both walk to the car. Cindy gets in and drives off. She sees all the sun in her face as she drives then she turns on the radio.**

Radio Announcer:

On this sad note, John F. Kennedy Jr., his wife Carolyn Bessette and sister in law Lauren Bessete has been found. John F. Kennedy Jr. was found in the cockpit and the sisters were found together underneath the plane... (Cindy hurries to turn off the radio. Reaches up to finally bring down the sun visor. We see her husband picture connected to the sun visor, and a baby picture of Bece and herself all together having fun.)

**\*In her head we hear.\***

Voice:

It's not your turn.

**\*(She puckers up her lips, lifts her two fingers to them to lay a kiss on the photo of Bart and the family.)\***

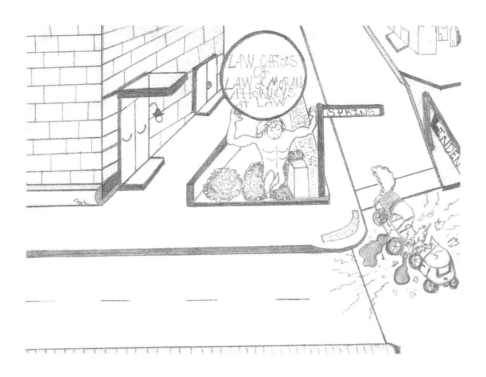

**WHAM!**

(We see Cindy's car being totaled out. We see her bracing herself for the worst. She's holding on to the steering wheel trying to control the car. She is biting her bottom lip so hard that the blood from her lip hits the camera. Then out of nowhere the car is calm and there is a bright light in front of Cindy. As this is going on we can hear loud car accidents sounds. We hear Like calling for Cindy.)

(1.) We see Eeshun and Day. Eeshun rises as if she knows that something has gone wrong.

(2.) Lady is still in the chair and this cold dreadful chill comes over her and she awakens.

(3.) Bece is asleep on Like's living room sofa and at this moment Melody comes home and Bece jumps up and looks at Melody, but as he looks at her she is looking just like Cindy. He shakes it off and he notices that it's not his mom.

(4.) As the camera comes back to the scene of the accident we hear and see all this chaos going on and here I am caught up in the middle of all this action.

Trish Spears:
I was in the back of the bartender's pick-up truck. No officer, I didn't get his name. I really can't explain what happen I just jumped up because I heard someone calling Cindy and I

knew that Cindy Chocolate was here last night. And I thought to myself not that Cindy. When I actually got to my knees I saw Like Waters was running up the street. I don't know why they were still here at this time of the morning. I'm just giving you my statement to the best of my knowledge if you need to know anything else you'll have to ask somebody else...

*(As the camera moves away from all the chaos it begins to go into the air pass the clouds and into the stars. Now it's the end of the film then we see rows of film reels all lined up across, straight up and down, it look like a big studio in heaven. The camera turns around one last time and we see Cindy right behind it blocking some of the light.

End of Film

# About the Author

The author, Debbie Lynn Lewis, writes:

"We never know who, what, and when our lives will be touched. What impact it will have after It's been touched… Things that happened and didn't happen in the past, with the things happening in my present was starting to bring sadness and grief to my heart. I believe in Love, beating the odds and letting things go to see will they return to me; but that doesn't mean time will stand still for us to capture all our dreams. I've made my decisions in life and I'm all right, but it's okay to dream and to ask "What If" I had one more try? Well, I did that, now I'm writing about the "one more chance" in life to do something else. The question is what will you do? I'm doing my "What If", I'm writing. I hope you enjoy my precious gift to you from above with continuous LOVE.. There's no greater gift without Thee.

D.L.L.

CPSIA information can be obtained
at www.ICGtesting.com
Printed in the USA
LVHW060119140323
741536LV00036B/2396